"Inspiring! Kristen Zavo teaches us how to navigate the pressures of our workaholic world, take charge of our own self-care, and achieve personal and professional fulfillment – that busyness is not a badge of honor – and to instead be purposeful and intentional."

~ Flavia Colgan, Director of Colgan Foundation and former Network News Commentator

"Wealth is not the accumulation of money; it is about happiness in everything you do, including work. Reading *Job Joy* will make you wealthy beyond your dreams."

~ Stephen Shapiro, author, *Best Practices are Stupid*

"Kristen demystifies the process of finding a job you love and her practical step-by-step guidance makes it easy to take the leap. Her encouraging words and her focus on mindset, boundaries, and self-care make it a must-read for women who are ready for MORE in their career. I loved her section on marketing yourself as a brand to find the right job for you. Her practical advice on how to increase your online presence and become more attractive to employers is gold."

~ Nicole Moore, Love Coach and Founder of Love Works

"Eventually, most of us end up settling in some part of our life. We let go of certain ideals and dreams; we compromise, and we make trade-offs. We gradually learn that we can't have everything we want, because not every outcome in life can be perfectly controlled. But if we pay close attention, we also learn that we can make the best of every outcome, and still get a lot of what we want in life, if we manage our time, energy and attitude appropriately.

And these realizations collectively lead to an interesting question: When should you settle, or compromise, and when should you continue fighting hard for what you ideally want to achieve?

Job Joy is smart, practical, authentic and will help you answer this question. Readers will finish the book with both clarity and a plan to make their career dreams a reality."

~ Angel Chernoff, Author and Coach,
Marc and Angel Hack Life

"The title says it all! Job Joy is full of powerful and practical tools to find more happiness and meaning in your work, whether that means changing jobs, starting a new career, or staying where you are. A must-read for anyone who is, or has ever felt, stuck in their career!"

~ Adam LoDolce, Founder of SexyConfidence.com

"*Job Joy* is a must-read, not just for people that are unhappy in their jobs, but for anyone looking to be more fulfilled in their life!! The author, Kristen Zavo, is definitely an expert and knows how to get results. She touches on every aspect of the process of finding joy, from self-reflection and goal setting, all the way to dealing with fears. I personally love my career as an entrepreneur but after reading this book, I have a list of things to do to make me a much more successful business owner! After reading *Job Joy*, I have more confidence in my decisions, a clearly defined vision of what success means in my life, and a plan to achieve much greater joy in my life!"

~ **Courtney Megan Hunt, Founder of Inspiration Bound**

"*Job Joy* is the perfect book for anyone that needs to do some reflection on their career and life. Kristen bares her soul and allows her readers to experience, through her eyes, the trials and tribulations in her own career. As a Mental Health Therapist, I love the way she pushes her readers to not only reflect and recognize needed life changes, but encourages them to take action!"

~ **Shari Goldsmith LISW, Founder, Workplace Resilience**

Job Joy

JOB JOY

Your Guide to Success, Meaning, and Happiness in Your Career

KRISTEN J. ZAVO

NEW YORK

LONDON • NASHVILLE • MELBOURNE • VANCOUVER

Job Joy

Your Guide to Success, Meaning and Happiness in Your Career

© 2019 Kristen J. Zavo

Published in New York, New York, by Morgan James Publishing in partnership with Difference Press. Morgan James is a trademark of Morgan James, LLC.
www.MorganJamesPublishing.com

ISBN 9781642792249 paperback
ISBN 9781642792256 eBook
Library of Congress Control Number: 2018955078

Cover and Interior Design by:
Chris Treccani
www.3dogcreative.net

Morgan James is a proud partner of Habitat for Humanity Peninsula and Greater Williamsburg. Partners in building since 2006.

Get involved today! Visit
MorganJamesPublishing.com/giving-back

For Mom (Mama Bear) and Dad. Thank you for always encouraging me to find my own path.

I love you.

FOREWORD

Happiness: we all seek it, in our life and in our work. It may look different for each of us, yet ultimately happiness comes down to being true to ourselves and aligning with a meaningful purpose.

Easier said than done, right? My quest for happiness, and purpose, has led to some great adventures: roles at Apple and Google, entrepreneurship, the honor of coaching amazing executives and teaching inspiring learners at Stanford and beyond.

Yet, like everyone, I've had moments when I've asked myself, "Is this actually what I'm here to be doing?" and "Am I making full use of my time and talents?" Somewhere inside, I knew – not always, but at key moments – I was missing that "something more."

These questions led me to explore the psychology and neuroscience of happiness, a topic I wrote about in a best-selling book and have shared on The Today Show and CNN, in publications including The New York Times, CNBC, Inc., and with audiences around the world. It was at an event in Cincinnati that I heard Kristen share her thoughts on "hacking happiness" – using intentional paths to create meaningful life changes that led to more satisfaction. Her insight into fulfillment, self-care, intentionality, and – well, simply being a healthy and real human – inspired me. She saw deeply into the insights I had explored on a theoretical level and made them practical, real-world, and available to all of us.

I connected with Kristen's passion to help high achievers channel their passion to connect with work they love. Challenging the usual assumptions about "career" and purpose, Kristen reminds us it's never too late to bring our whole selves to the work we do – or to reclaim our truth in ways that improve our relationships, health, and overall wellbeing.

Jump in. You'll be inspired by Kristen's personal story and by her insights on redefining your relationship with work (spoiler alert: YOU are in charge. Work isn't), real-world examples, and 100% achievable principles for building a career that combines success, meaning, and joy.

As I wrote in *The Happiness Hack*, "You matter. As do your contributions, whatever they may be." Kristen will remind you in the pages to come that you deserve, and can have, a career that excites you, inspires you, and delivers the fulfillment that comes from meaningful work. Take these words to heart. Guided by Job Joy, you'll find new paths to sharing your unique gifts, bringing to the world the talents and authenticity that set a new standard for what work can be – and for what the world needs now.

Congratulations on the first step.

Ellen Petry Leanse
Author, *The Happiness Hack*
Chief People Officer, Lucidworks
Neuroscience Educator and Technology Pioneer

TABLE OF CONTENTS

Introduction

Job: a regular remunerative position; a specific duty, role
Joy: the emotion evoked by well-being, success, good
fortune, or by the prospect of possessing what one
desires; a state of happiness; a source of delight
~ MERRIAM-WEBSTER DICTIONARY

L ife is too short to dread going to the office each morning, to not do meaningful work, to not love what you do. Yet so many of us spend way too many hours at our jobs, doing work that isn't fulfilling while sacrificing the rest of our lives – our health, well-being, family, friendships, and romantic relationships.

Why do we do this? Well, for one: the paycheck. And because we feel it's too late, and too much work, to change. After all, if you've been doing the same thing for 5, 10, 15-plus years, the thought of doing anything else can be crippling. This is what you went to school for. And what you're good at! And you make great money! And in this economy, you'd be crazy to consider anything different! And then you resign yourself to working at a job you don't love (maybe don't even like) because that's what adults do. Most people don't like their jobs anyway, right?

Further complicating the issue is how you can be successful by all traditional measures – having the title, income, and impressive résumé – but still not be happy. For some, traditional success is enough. Many of us want more. We want our work to have meaning, to make a difference. We simply spend too many hours on the job to settle for anything less.

Imagine how it would feel to love your work – not just survive it – but to really enjoy what you do and know that it matters. To wake up in the morning and be excited to start your day. Your first meeting doesn't start until after lunch because you know you get your best work done in the first few hours of the day, and you have the flexibility and control over your schedule to protect those precious hours. Then you step out of the office (which may be your home) to have lunch. If it's a nice afternoon, maybe you sit on a park bench and take a few moments to eat without distraction. Or maybe you meet a potential business partner and, over salads, discuss how to bring a new service or product to market, one that you know will make it even easier for your clients to solve their problems with you.

Then back to the office for calls and meetings, all of which start with a clear purpose and end with next steps, responsible parties, and a timeline. Before you know it, it's time to plan for tomorrow before you head out of the office. You're usually out by 6 p.m. to make it to the gym, but today is Wednesday, and you've got dinner plans with your significant other. You've committed to at least one midweek date night to make sure you stay connected throughout the week. Depending on what's going on at work, you might check email once before settling in for the night. Then you indulge in some bad TV or a little light reading before bed. You end the day feeling connected, productive, and grateful.

Does any of that sound good? If you are excited at the thought of experiencing joy in your work, you're in the right place. I so get where you're at. I've been where you are now, multiple times, whether my ultimate decision was to stay put, change jobs, or completely change careers. It wasn't always easy, but it was always worth it. As the years went by, friends, colleagues, and team members started asking me how I did it. Everyone's specific situation was different, but they all had something in common – despite having successful careers, they were unhappy. In a world where we are taught to be grateful, some even thought something was wrong with them for feeling the way they did. Worse, they believed there was nothing they could do to change their situation. It is my belief that there is nothing further from the truth.

In the pages that follow, I'll share my experiences and client stories – as well as the steps my clients and I took to find meaning and fulfillment in our work. This guide is broken up into three sections: Reflect, Decide, and Act. At the end of each chapter you'll find a summary, or what I call "Joy Notes" – the three to five most important takeaways and action items to get started on now.

In the Reflect chapters, you'll start by getting real about how you got to this place and what it's costing you. You'll redefine success, on your own terms, regardless of whether that definition fits what society, your friends, or your parents tell you.

In the Decide section, you'll find ways to make the best of your current situation – to be happy and find meaning now. With greater self-awareness, it's time to make some decisions, to lay out your options and build a plan for your long-term career happiness.

The last, and most important section is about Action. In these chapters, I'll share my steps, tips, and resources for changing jobs and even careers. No matter how great a plan you have, it can be difficult to do what is necessary to make the change you so desire. So we'll look at the top fears that may be holding you back and ways to overcome those challenges. Finally, we'll learn how it's all connected and explore ways to find meaning and happiness both at and outside of work.

It's never too late to change, and to take control of your career again. It's time to move beyond hollow success to a place where your work brings you meaning, fulfillment, and joy. You've got this! It's time to find your job joy!

PART 1

Reflect

The more reflective you are, the more effective you are.

~ HALL AND SIMERAL

CHAPTER ONE

I Can't Get No Satisfaction
My Story

The only way to do great work is to love what you do.
If you haven't found it yet, keep looking. Don't settle.
~ STEVE JOBS

Growing up, success generally came easy for me. Yes, I studied and worked hard, but I always got straight As and was at the top of my class. I graduated high school in three years, received my Bachelor of Science with two majors and a minor, a couple weeks before my 20th birthday, and continued on to earn my MBA in finance by the age of 21. While in college and grad school, I taught test prep classes, teaching high school kids not far from my own age, as well as grad students, some easily twice my age. After graduating, I continued teaching but got my first "real" job in banking, where I was responsible for monitoring the financial performance of a portfolio of real estate entities. By all outside measures, I was successful.

But just a few months into my new job, I started to get restless – a feeling that would become very familiar to me as I progressed in my career. I had what seemed like good reasons. For someone accustomed to progressing fast and on my own timeline, the traditional banking method of promoting based on tenure instead of performance, frustrated me. And as was the nature of portfolio management, I reported to a handful of managers, who understandably each deemed their work to be top priority – a seemingly unwinnable position for me. But in retrospect, I now know it was deeper than that, and something I didn't want to face. I was questioning if my work mattered. In this particular instance, since my portfolio consisted of successful, blue chip companies, I suspected that my analysis was more of a "check the box" item for the bank – and that no matter what, these companies would continue to get their requested credit line increases and loans.

After just one year, I started looking for another job. This was unheard of at the time. Even to this day, we have this idea that you can't leave a company until you've been there at least three years – especially if it's your first job out of school. But I was young, had chutzpah, and hadn't invested years in my career yet.

I left banking for the world of consulting, working for a firm that specialized in distressed businesses and restructurings – quite the opposite of the companies in my portfolio at the bank. At first, it was exciting. I traveled every week to client sites, worked hard all day, and then had dinners out (expensed of course!) at night with my new colleagues and friends. But about a year in, I started to get that restless feeling again. I had different reasons this time. The 12-hour days were getting to me, as was the travel. Because I was on the road all the time, my home office didn't know me, which was bad for politics and promotions. And again, it was more than just these surface issues. I started to doubt the difference my work was making. Sure, I was learning a ton, billing lots of hours, and making good money. But I questioned if my work actually mattered, and if our clients actually implemented and maintained the changes we suggested – or if it went back to business-as-usual as soon as we left. I suspected the latter and it didn't feel good.

Still, I loved consulting, so I decided to join a top firm known for interim management. Unlike many consulting firms that were known for coming in, analyzing the problems, presenting a solution, and then leaving – this firm actually implemented the plans they recommended. This satisfied my initial desire for meaning and I stayed there, got promoted, and took on more challenging projects, traveling the country for seven years. But if I'm honest, it was probably at least three years too long. After a few years in, I had a full roster of former clients that I kept in touch with. I began to notice that many continued to struggle with the same issues they hired us for, long after we were gone, despite the initial implementation and management we had done for them. The "interim management" distinction in the field of consulting didn't seem to be making the difference I had thought it would.

But something was different this time. It wasn't as easy to leave as it had been in my previous two jobs. Something they don't tell you at the start of many successful careers is that once you make it past a few years, you get your very own pair of golden handcuffs. At first, you might not even notice they're there. It starts out innocently enough. You like your job. You get paid well, very well in some cases. You sign a lease for a nice, overpriced apartment or buy a house with a mortgage you can barely afford. You are overworked and stressed, so you find ways to treat yourself, because you deserve it! Maybe you enjoy expensive dinners out with friends, afternoons at the spa, or shopping for designer brand clothes (you are no stranger to red-bottomed shoes). And it makes you feel better, for the moment anyway. And then you wake up one day and you have this lifestyle that you've become accustomed to, that you can't imagine changing.

Plus, by now you've invested what feels like so much time building your career in a particular industry. On top of that, leaving also means losing out financially, and not just to maintain your current lifestyle but to receive what you've already earned. You may be waiting for payout from last year's bonus, and/or biding your time for your options to be fully vested. This is a vicious cycle, because the longer you stay, the more dollars are at risk.

So I stayed. I moved to New York City, where I lived in a high-rise doorman building. I indulged in designer clothes and luxury brand shoes. (If I was going to hate my job, I figured I might as well feel good in my clothes.) I bought the best in skincare and makeup products, and in my free time, worked out at overpriced boutique gyms where $35 for a 45-minute class was the norm. Since I worked six to seven days a week and ten to twelve hour days, there wasn't time for much more. Work, workout, work some more, eat, sleep, repeat.

To an outsider, I had it all – a successful career, an impressive résumé, a great wardrobe, an expensive New York City lifestyle, and a job that allowed me to travel all over the country (and earn all those frequent flier miles!). But I wasn't happy. I wasn't passionate about my work. I had that nagging feeling that what I was doing didn't matter (at least not to me). All of this led to what I'll call my 30th birthday breakdown.

I've never been one to make a big deal out of birthdays, and this one was no exception. The day was fine, nothing exceptional really. But that night, I woke up from a dream, extremely upset and hysterically crying. This was out of character for me. After almost a decade working in a male-dominated field, I had trained – and prided myself – in not being emotional. This night was different. I called my mom in the middle of the night (of course), and she listened as I went on and on between sobs. There were so many thoughts going through my head.

This is not where I expected to be at 30.
I'm not happy.
I don't feel successful.
More often than not, I don't like what I am doing.
I am burned out.
I look at my managers and their managers, and don't like what I see in my future if I stay.

How did I get here? How can I get out?
It is too late! Almost ten years in, I'm too far along in my career to change. What can I do?

My mom and I didn't solve my problems that night. Actually, I would put off taking action for almost two more years, waiting for a health crisis to knock some sense into me and to give me the perspective I needed to completely change careers (more on that later).

I share my story to show you that I understand and have been in your situation. I have built a successful career, only to feel unhappy and unfulfilled, craving more meaning but feeling stuck and at a loss as to what to do next. And I've gotten through what feels like an insurmountable challenge, to the other side.

I also know what it's like to feel excited and inspired by the work you do, and who you get to do it with. To know that the work you do is aligned with your values and makes a difference. To have a job that makes you feel successful, happy, and on purpose.

It took six jobs, three career changes, and compromised health and happiness for me to figure out what was missing in my career and how to change it. I don't want you to have to endure the same. That is why I wrote this book.

My hope is that it will help you speed up this process, so that you can experience success, meaning, and happiness in your career faster - and make the difference you are meant to make sooner - in the lives of the clients and customers you serve, and more importantly, in your own life and the lives of your loved ones.

JOY NOTES

- If you find yourself unhappy and unfulfilled despite a successful career, you are not alone.
- You do not need to sacrifice your happiness or fulfillment in order to be successful
- This guide will provide you with strategies and tools to find success, meaning, and happiness in your career.

CHAPTER TWO

All I Want Is to Have My Peace of Mind
Redefining Success

Now you're climbin' to the top of the company ladder
Hope it doesn't take too long
Can'tcha you see there'll come a day when it won't matter?
Come a day when you'll be gone
~ BOSTON, "PEACE OF MIND"

The goal of this chapter is threefold: first, to help you understand where you are and how you got here; second, to clearly articulate what it is costing you; and third, to examine your definition of success. I want you to move from feelings of frustration and overwhelm with your current situation to a place of understanding, confidence, and hope.

If you skip this self-reflection, you could end up spinning your wheels – and even if you do make a change, it will likely not have the lasting impact you are seeking. Let me explain.

About a year before my 30th birthday breakdown, I was clear on a few things. I was unhappy. I didn't like where I was in my career. I needed a change. But at that point, I didn't spend the time to figure out how I got there or the deeper reason I was so unhappy. What I did do was decide to embark on a minimum three-year path to attain my CFA (Chartered Financial Analyst designation). For anyone who has been through that, or knows someone who has, you know it is a super strenuous, highly regarded, self-study program with three tests spread over the course of three years. It is arguably more difficult than earning an MBA, with a pass rate of around 35 percent for each test. People give up their life for the three to six months before the exam for intense study.

Looking back, this was an interesting choice for me to make, especially since I ultimately realized I didn't want a career solely in finance. At the time though, it felt good to take action, however uninspired. My thought was I'd get the certification and then be able to get a better, higher paying job. Except my problem wasn't that I didn't have a good enough job or that I wasn't paid enough. It was that *despite* having a good job and good pay, I wasn't fulfilled or happy in my career.

Around the same time, I remember having conversations with Alicia, a friend and colleague of mine who worked for one of my clients. Her role was in the finance department. She confided in me that she hated every second of it. The people were okay, but the work was not at all what she wanted to do. So I was surprised when Alicia told me she was considering going back for a graduate degree – in finance. When you are on the outside looking in, it can seem so obvious. Why on earth would you go back for a degree in the one subject you know you dislike? Well to her, it made perfect sense. This was the career she had chosen, so even though she didn't like it, she might as well continue her education and rise up the corporate ladder in the industry. I thought she was crazy, and yet here I was doing the same thing.

The point? Taking action for action's sake may feel good in the moment, but gets you nowhere and wastes precious time that you could be spending on building a career that makes you happy.

It was a couple years in before I came to this realization and stopped pursuing the CFA. If I had been honest with myself and gotten clear on not just why I was unhappy, but what I desired in my career, then I never would have wasted the time, money, and energy studying for a certification that I was not interested in using. I could have been that much closer to having the job that I wanted.

I don't want you to make the same mistake.

Get Real About Your Current Work Situation

Understanding where you are and how you got here will help ensure that, unlike me, you don't stay in a job that isn't for you, and that your next move is aligned with your current goals. You want to avoid, as the old saying goes, jumping out of the frying pan and into the fire. There's nothing worse than leaving one miserable job for another that is just as miserable, but with the additional challenges of learning a new company, culture, and way of working.

You can't find a cure for your job dissatisfaction if you aren't clear on the cause. I want you to take some serious time to understand exactly what it is about your job that is making you less than excited to go to work. So get out your journal or notepad, open up a new note on your phone, or bring up a fresh Word doc on your laptop and think about how you feel about the following:

- Your actual day-to-day work
- Your workload (too much, too little)
- The work environment – location, work arrangement (closed v. open layout, cubes v. offices), etc.
- The people you work with and who you report to
- The culture, politics, work ethic
- Upward and lateral mobility, or lack thereof
- The hours, commute, amount of travel
- How much of your answers above are inherent to your department, your company, and your industry?

If I had answered these questions earlier, I would have said that while I did enjoy some parts of the work (strategy, business plans, presentations), I despised the majority of my day-to-day reality – data entry, small creditor negotiations, and making endless edits to PowerPoint presentations that no one was going to look at anyway. I valued productivity and efficiency and craved more time outside of work.

But the industry tended to attract workaholics who were hiding in their work to escape their personal lives. I'll never forget my surprise when a newly engaged coworker told me he would leave the house before 5 a.m. to catch a flight, hours earlier than necessary, just so he could have some quiet time away from his soon-to-be wife and work in "peace." I still remember my shock, and how I knew in that moment that not only did I never want to become that person, but I didn't want to marry one either.

In today's culture, this kind workaholism behavior is often rewarded – in some places more so than others. Rewards come in a variety of forms – whether actual money, promotions, or simply the approval of our superiors and peers. Plus, there's no denying that there is a badge of honor and pride that goes with working long hours.

I remember talking about this exact issue with Catherine, a client of mine who is a lawyer in Manhattan. She told me about a time earlier in her career that shaped how she thought about working long hours. Fresh out of law school, working as a first-year associate in a boutique New York City law firm, she remembered receiving a surprise in the mail in early June. It was a business book with a $100 bill in it from the head of the firm, with a note thanking her for working (billing) hours on Memorial Day. She felt pretty darn special then, and it no doubt encouraged her to continue working on holidays and weekends, and to take pride in doing so.

Fast forward a few years, and this once passionate and ambitious lawyer was at her wit's end, fantasizing about marrying so she could quit her job. That was unlike her, but she was burned out and now it was affecting other parts of her life. She had gained weight, was on blood pressure pills as a result of the stress, and was definitively single. The thought of finding time to date with her current work schedule was laughable. By the time we started working together, Catherine had become jaded and cynical, to the point of not recognizing herself.

All of this is not to say that hard work isn't necessary. It is. You wouldn't be where you are today without it. But when it gets to a point that it affects your health and well-being, it's time to review priorities. We've all heard about the top deathbed regrets; some are memorably recorded and made popular by Bronnie Ware on her blog "Inspiration and Chai." At the end of their lives, people don't wish they had accomplished more and made more money. Instead, they regret working so much, not being true to themselves, and not allowing themselves to be happy.

Understand How You Got Here

While you're doing the work to get real about your current situation, it also makes sense to understand how and why you got to this place. There are lots of reasons we end up where we do. Maybe in your case, your parents nudged (pushed) you in a certain direction. Maybe you are trying to live up to their ideal vision of you and you don't want to let them down. Maybe you fell into your job, and the momentum of life is responsible for where you are today. Or perhaps when you went to school, you weren't sure what you wanted to do, so you chose something that seemed okay and made a career out of it.

It could also be that your job, company, or industry changed. And you were holding out hope that it would get better and return to the days you remember loving. Or it could be that you, your circumstances, or priorities changed – so that the job that once was so fulfilling is now just a source of stress.

There are lots of drivers behind our career choices, some conscious, some unconscious. For me, it was about continuing the success I had experienced in school, and that meant striving for, and maintaining, a career in a prestigious industry, with an impressive title and a hefty paycheck. If I'm honest, I also wanted to be successful because I wanted to make my parents proud. And I can see now that on a deeper level, I based my self-worth on my accomplishments. If I wasn't climbing the corporate ladder, working more hours, meeting important people, and making more money, then I was a disappointment to everyone including – and especially – myself.

Our society is addicted to productivity.
We think productivity increases our value as a human.
And we want to be valued and loved.
So… we become addicted to productivity.
~ Danielle LaPorte

Acknowledge What It's Costing You

Now that you are clear on where you are, and how you got here, it's time to be honest with yourself about what it is costing you.

As I said earlier, it took me almost two years from the point I realized I was unhappy until I finally left the job and career that was sucking the soul out of me. The main reason it took so long was because I wasn't honest with myself about why I was so unhappy and how I got there. It took a health scare to get me there.

About six months after my birthday breakdown, I started to get terrible headaches. I would easily pop ten plus Tylenol or Motrin in a day. And then that stopped working. I am not the type of person that runs to the doctor for every ache and pain, but now my headaches were interfering with my ability to work the long hours I had become accustomed to, and I couldn't have that.

After seeing a few specialists to no avail, I went to a neurologist who specialized in headaches and who told me that I had migraines. After our initial consultation, the doctor sat me down for a firm talk. She told me point blank that my work lifestyle was causing this, and that it was putting my health at risk. She told me that I needed eight hours of sleep, ten minutes of sunshine (for natural vitamin D) and healthy, chemical-free food.

I remember literally laughing out loud – at all of it, but especially at the sleep. I was now on a traveling project where we worked all day in a windowless conference room, got takeout for dinner and brought it back to our hotel rooms, and then worked a couple more hours. Emails after midnight were not unusual. And I couldn't "just leave" in the middle of the day for a ten-minute break to take a walk in the fresh air. As I write this now, it seems ridiculous. But that was my truth at that point.

Among the prescriptions for a myriad of pills and nasal sprays, I left that day with a prescription for "eight hours of sleep." As if I could ever show that to my manager. Needless to say, I didn't get relief from my headaches during that project.

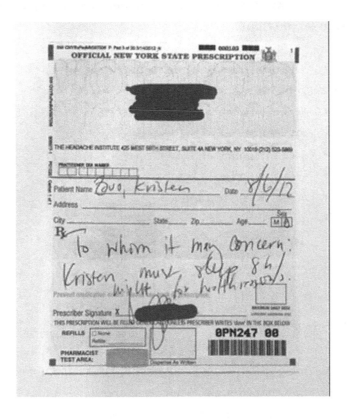

It became clear to me that leaving my current job was not just about finding work I enjoyed. The workload, environment, and culture were affecting my health and well-being. While the situation and specific health effects were different, the same was true for Catherine whose weight and blood pressure – not to mention, romantic life – were suffering.

What is your current situation costing you? Pull out your journal, notes app, or Word doc and spend at least 20 minutes thinking about it. Feel free to come back to this list over a period of a week as more comes to mind. Here is a high-level list to get you thinking:

- Opportunity cost: time spent at work missing out on other things
- Financial cost: staying at a job without promotions and pay increases that you deserve
- Health: mental and emotional
- Health: physical
- A life! Happiness and joy
- Peace of mind (always stressed)
- Time with family and friends
- Love, relationships
- Basic self-care

Redefine Success

We know what traditional measures of success are, and I'd be willing to bet that you have achieved most, if not all, of them. But is that enough? What does success mean to you?

While in my consulting career, most would agree that I had achieved success. But I was working around the clock, felt terrible with my nonstop migraines, and had very little time for friendships. I was in constant go-go-go mode, which in a way, was good, because if I stopped, I would realize how bad I felt.

When I lived in New York City, I would go to mass at a beautiful little chapel in the middle of Times Square. I found a lot of comfort there, as it was the one place and time that I could be quiet and not "do" without feeling guilty. (Who can argue with God coming first?) One Sunday afternoon as I sat in mass, tears suddenly started rolling down my cheeks. And then, full on, snot-inducing, muffled, ugly-crying waterworks. I was mortified and dumbfounded. I didn't understand why I was crying. All I knew was that I felt a deep sadness that I hadn't been able to feel when I was constantly in "on" mode. This was the day that it hit me. I knew that something had to change and that if this was what success looked like, I wanted no part of it.

I longed for more freedom, to work on projects and tasks that mattered, to feel appreciated on the job, and to have more time outside of it – to have more happiness, joy, love, and adventure that can only come from living with more balance in life.

So what is success to you? I want you to dig deep and be honest with yourself here.

- Besides money and title, what else does success mean to you?
- What would make you love your job? (e.g. money, title, different work, more flexibility)
- Think about your list of what your job is costing you – could some of that define success?

- What are your top priorities in life? Is the life you live now aligned with what you say those priorities are?
- Allow yourself to dream. If you could do anything, what would be your perfect day? Maybe at first it would be laying on a beach, getting massages and reading romance novels. But you're so driven, that would only satisfy you for so long. So what would it look like if it included work? What would you do? Where would you work – from home, in an office, at a coffee shop, a combination of all three? Who would you work with – solo or on a team? When would you start and end work? What else would you have time for in your day?
- If there were no judgment (from you or anyone else), what would success look like to you?

Just as you will change, the things that make you happy and fulfilled will change. It is normal to redefine success every few years. Maybe you're like Catherine who started with a traditional definition of success, where graduating law school, passing the bar, and working as an associate at a Manhattan firm felt good. But as she gained more experience and growth, she found herself wishing for love and romance and to dial back the work schedule. Success at work was no longer enough. She sought more balance and deeper relationships. Ultimately, she wanted a partnership and a family, and she realized that if her work situation didn't change that would be nearly impossible. Yet it wasn't until she recognized this change within herself that she was able to build a plan to meet her new definition of success, which for her meant finding a new job that allowed her the time to focus on non-work priorities.

Recent generations have successfully challenged the belief that women should be content solely with marriage and a family, arguing that career success is a goal worthy of pursuit as part of a full life. And yet, for all the progress made here, one unforeseen effect is that many women now feel ashamed if career *isn't* their be-all and end-all. I have found that some of even the most ambitious and successful businesswomen are feeling this way, but afraid to act on it or even say it out loud. So I'll say it for you. Your career does not need to have a leading role, or *any* role for that matter, in your definition of success. It is okay to desire to be a stay-at-home mom, or to have your work just be a means of funding the rest of your amazing life.

Whatever your definition of success is, admitting it to yourself and then taking action to achieve it, can be one of the most courageous and rewarding things you ever do. That is why the questions in this chapter are not meant to be answered quickly. The good news is that no answer is wrong as long as it is true to you. It is so important to take your time, to be honest with yourself and get clear, so that you can make decisions from a place of deep self-knowing. Clarity around that which you want to change will allow you to direct your energy toward your desired future, and more specifically, to determine definitive next steps for your unique situation.

That's all good and fine, you say – but I'm miserable now! How will I survive in the short-term? I've got you covered. Sometimes before we can focus on an exit plan, we need to build a survival plan. In the next chapter, we'll look at five areas where you can take action now to make your work life more bearable and – gasp – even pleasant.

JOY NOTES

- Self-reflection before action is paramount to your success.
- Action for action's sake wastes time and keeps you from experiencing fulfillment at work.
- Avoid repeating mistakes by taking the time to understand your work situation, how you got here, and what it's costing you.
- In order to be successful, you must move beyond traditional definitions and clearly articulate what success means to you.
- Self-awareness and a clear vision of success allow for intentional, aligned action – getting you to your goal faster.

PART 2

Decide

Decision is the ultimate power. Decisions shape destiny.
~ TONY ROBBINS

CHAPTER THREE

Come On, Get Happy
Finding Happiness at Work Now

The key to happiness is the decision to be happy.
~ MARIANNE WILLIAMSON

According to a 2017 Gallup poll, 85 percent of people hate their jobs. That doesn't have to be you. In this chapter, we'll explore ways to make life more bearable at work now, before we even consider longer-term steps that could involve changing jobs or even careers.

Whether you stay in your current role for another month, a couple years, or indefinitely, these strategies will help you cope with stress, avoid burnout and make the best of your work situation. There are countless ways to improve your happiness immediately, which I've grouped into five categories: boundaries, self-care, productivity, mindset, and actively seeking joy. They are all related and build upon each other, but even choosing just one area to focus on can make a huge difference in your day-to-day happiness.

Set Boundaries

Before we get into boundaries, I want to share Marie's experience with boundaries at work. She now works in product development at a start-up, but when I met her, she was a consultant like me. Also like me, she had a tough time saying no. This is the story of how she reached her limit and what happened next.

For months, Marie had been traveling every week, Monday through Thursday from Boston to a remote client site in Minnesota. The job was only supposed to last a couple months, but had been extended twice with no end in sight. Twelve-hour days, six to seven days a week, were the norm. One Thursday night when she and her team were scheduled to fly home, after multiple delays, their flights were cancelled. They got on the waitlist for the last flight out, but because she did not have status on this particular airline, everyone on her team except her made it home that night.

Marie stayed at an airport hotel for the night, but had no toiletries or clean clothes. (In order to travel lighter, when traveling to the same site every week, it was the norm to leave toiletries and even some clothes at the base hotel.) When she finally arrived home the next morning, she was tired, cranky, and in the same clothes as the day before. Understandably, she couldn't wait to get in the shower. As she walked into her apartment, her boss texted her to confirm her participation on a call – without even asking if she was okay and had arrived home safely.

Marie's normal response would have been to get on the call no matter what. She didn't like to disappoint and was afraid of pushing back against her manager's demands. But this time was different. In that moment, she made the courageous and rebellious decision to put down the phone, take a shower, and miss the call.

The world didn't end when Marie stood up for herself and her needs. After getting settled at home, she simply called her manager and got caught up on the call. Over a year later and still in the same job, Marie told me that that day changed everything. She had reached her breaking point, and from then on, she started setting boundaries – little by little, and on everything from the times she was available to work, to the flights she would take. Contrary to what she would have believed earlier, she was just as, if not more, respected now that she stood up for herself.

Can you relate to any part of Marie's experience? Many of us have found success by being people-pleasers, going above and beyond what was asked of us (or needed), and putting ourselves – and even our most basic needs – last. This is not only a disservice to you, but also to those around you, including the people you work with. We've all heard the flight announcement that, in case of emergency, put on your own oxygen mask before helping others. That applies here, too. If you aren't taking care of yourself, you can't bring your best self to the job – which is ironically the very reason you tell yourself you can't eat lunch, leave by 6 p.m., or in Marie's case, even take a shower.

Boundaries allow us to take better care of ourselves mentally, physically, and emotionally. You, like Marie, may be surprised to find that the world doesn't end when you set them. You might have some difficult conversations, yes. But ultimately, you will feel better and be respected more than those who do not set boundaries.

This means something different for each of us. Perhaps for you, it could be around workload and work schedule. If you are working ten-hour days and then going home and working more, either you're not productive (which we'll talk about later), or you have way too much work to do. If that's the case and there's no end in sight, then it's time to reevaluate your tasks, the time spent on them, and their value – and based on that, determine what should be the priority. This might necessitate a conversation with your manager and team to re-prioritize your projects, delegate responsibilities, and even altogether stop some of your tasks.

While boundaries may need to be set around the actual time you are at the office, an even more common issue is about limiting the hours that you are "on" and reachable. If you're like most people, you always have your phone on you. According to a 2015 study by Deloitte, the average American checks their phone 46 times per day. If you're on the younger side, I'd be willing to bet it's even more. What this means is that when you're at work, you're thinking of all the things you'd rather be doing. And when you finally leave, you can't enjoy the activity and company around you, because you're just thinking of work.

Everyone needs time away from work to decompress, even if you're happy at your job – and especially if you're not. Checking your phone during dinner, on the treadmill, in bed, and at all hours of the night, does not make you a more productive employee. It makes you a stressed out, exhausted robot that is incapable of being present in the moment. I know I have had to ask myself if I was okay taking a call from my boss at 10 p.m. at night. And sometimes I was, but most of the time, the answer was no. You'll have to determine what makes the most sense for your particular situation and time in your life, but whatever you decide – communicate and stick to it.

It doesn't necessarily mean you need to have an official conversation with anyone. It could be as simple as just turning off your phone and email notifications after a certain time and then responding the next morning. If you are questioned about it, you can casually say that you've found you can be more productive when you take a few hours off work at night to reset. Then set expectations by saying when you plan to be offline, and how you can be reached in case of emergency. People will learn that if they want a quicker response, they've got to contact you during business hours.

If you're still doubting your ability to put down your phone and close your laptop, consider that Sheryl Sandberg, COO at Facebook, commits to leaving the office by 5:30 p.m. every day. It doesn't mean that you can't get online later and quickly scan emails, but the idea is that you have a life outside of work and the ability to disconnect. You get this by setting boundaries.

Beyond workload and hours at the office, setting boundaries could also mean only accepting meeting invites where the purpose and your role are clear. Or it could be the scandalous act of taking lunch. Start with some easy wins and work your way up to setting boundaries in the bigger areas that feel more high risk – and likely, where you are being taken the most advantage of. If you can learn to set boundaries, it will raise your confidence, help you do your job better, and allow you to spend time on some non-work priorities.

Take Care of Yourself

Related to setting boundaries, but deserving of its own section, is self-care. I think most of us would agree that the more overwhelmed, stressed, and unhappy we are, the more we need to take care of ourselves. So why is it then, that basic self-care is the first thing to go when life gets crazy? When I say self-care, I'm not talking about booking spa appointments or a retreat in the mountains. While that is amazing, what I am referring to here is very basic – as in how you would care for a dog.

If you have a dog now, or had one growing up, you know that she needs regular exercise, good food, enough sleep, and plenty of play. You would never think of denying her those basics just because you got busy. Some might even call it animal cruelty to do so. Yet I am willing to bet that you deny yourself these very same essentials. I remember hearing this comparison one day and how it hit a little too close to home for me. It was one of the many times I was on the crazy train to burnout – and thinking of self-care from this perspective knocked some sense into me. *Would I really treat a dog better than I was treating myself?*

Physical, emotional, and mental health are essential – not just to be happy now, but to be able to handle life's challenges head on. No matter your situation, everything is worse when you're hungry, dead tired, and strung out on caffeine.

In her two most recent books, *Thrive* and *The Sleep Revolution*, Arianna Huffington stresses the need to recharge regularly so that we can come to work reinvigorated, with a clear mind and of sound judgment. This is true not just for work, but also for your overall well-being. Basic self-care will help you feel better now, and will also give you the energy and mental strength if and when you decide to look for a job.

With that in mind, it's time to ask yourself if you are taking care of your own basic needs:

- **Sleep:** It is common knowledge that adults need seven to nine hours of sleep each night. While we can survive on less, consistently running on a deficit puts us in a bad mood and makes things harder because it's more of a struggle to think clearly – affecting not just our work, but our relationships and overall happiness. In fact, multiple studies have shown that sleep deprivation causes performance similar to that of an intoxicated person. Do yourself (and those around you) a favor and commit to a minimum of seven hours of sleep on most nights.

- **Movement:** I intentionally didn't call this section "exercise." Not only does it hold a negative charge for some of us, but it can also imply specific activities and feel like just one more obligation on your to-do list. I believe that we should think of moving our bodies as something we *get* to do, not have to do. It's good for us physically, yes – but also great for our mind and soul. It helps us clear the cobwebs, get out of our head and feel more alive. And it doesn't have to be at a gym – it can be a walk around the block while catching up with girlfriends (on the phone or in person) or an impromptu dance party in your living room.

  In addition to regular exercise (movement), it's important to move throughout your day. As the 2017 study published in Annals of Internal Medicine, *Patterns of Sedentary Behavior and Mortality in U.S. Middle-Aged and Older Adults,* showed there is a direct relationship between sitting for prolonged periods of time and risk of early death. Set a timer for each hour and take a break, even if it's just a walk to the bathroom or around the floor. Find easy ways to sneak activity in by parking further from the door and experimenting with walking meetings at work.

- **Quality Food:** Stress eating is common in times of high stress. Bad-for-you snacks and caffeine can give you energy in the short-term, and for many of us, can be the only thing to look forward to in a busy day. While it may feel good in the short-term, skimping on high quality foods in favor of processed goodies can do a number on both our emotions and waistline. Along with more sleep and exercise, simply recognizing this pattern can go a long way in changing your behavior. In addition, think of ways you can plan ahead – that might mean having a good breakfast, bringing in leftovers, or having healthy snacks on hand.

- **Meditation:** Even just a few minutes of quiet time a day can help with anxiety and stress levels. If you are new to meditating, there is a plethora of information out there on various styles and techniques. Don't let that overwhelm you. It can be as simple as sitting up in bed for the first 5 minutes of your day with your eyes closed (or on the floor, against the wall, if you think you'll fall back asleep).

  I like to listen to music while I meditate – "Calm Meditation" or "Gregorian Chant" channels on Pandora are my favorites. Although typical advice is to let your thoughts go, I keep a notepad nearby for those that I simply must write down (I've gotten some great ideas during early morning meditations when my mind is still in a dream-like state). If you do this, just make sure to get right back to meditating.

- **Bonus Points! Morning Routine:** One way to make self-care a habit is to create a morning ritual. Although it can be, a morning routine doesn't have to be fancy or long. It's simply a way to start your day on the right foot with some quiet time and connection with yourself.

If this idea is new to you, I suggest starting with three activities – journaling, reading, and meditation – in any order and for any amount of time you choose. For example, I aim for at least five minutes of each but on particularly busy days I might only do 1 minute each. No matter how busy you are, you can at least give yourself three minutes a day! On slower days and weekends, I might do 30 minutes each of journaling and reading, and ten minutes of meditation. Try this for one week and see the difference it makes. I suspect you'll go through your day calmer and more centered than usual and better able to handle the day's challenges.

After a while, you'll learn to feel into what you need each day and make your morning ritual your own. Maybe you'll add having a cup of lemon tea, doing some light yoga, or reciting affirmations to your routine. Like runners that don't feel right on days they don't work out, you may even surprise yourself and look forward to this "me" time, missing it on those days when you sleep in.

Increase Productivity

If you're going to prioritize self-care and set boundaries around work, then you need to make sure that the hours you are at work are super productive. We've all heard and experienced the old adage or Parkinson's Law that states that *work expands so as to fill the time available for its completion.* It especially applies when you're doing work that you don't like – or in a place, or with people, you don't care for. When you hate your job, it is natural to do anything to procrastinate, whether that's playing on Facebook, gossiping with coworkers, or taking long lunches. But when you've decided to commit to being at work for a set period of time, you'll have to use that time wisely – to work while at work, so that you can *not* work when you're not there.

You'll find that if you know that you're leaving by a certain time, you'll get your work done faster and make those late nights the exception, not the rule. Especially at the beginning, it can help to plan something after work. If you have tickets to a show, dinner with a friend, or a yoga class that you've already paid for, you're more likely to be super productive so that you can leave on time.

To that end, below are five of my favorite productivity tips:

1. **Minimize meetings.**

    Countless surveys and studies show that in addition to wasting time and money, meetings impact productivity and happiness. In my last corporate job, it was not uncommon to have seven hours of scheduled time in one day, making it nearly impossible to get any actual work done at work.

    If you can, I suggest declining meetings where the purpose and your role are unclear, or at least clarifying those items before attending. Ask yourself if you can send another team member, or if the whole team was invited, which one of you it makes most sense to attend. If you're the one guilty of sending out those meeting invites, take the time to consider if an email would suffice. If not, maybe a shorter meeting with a tighter agenda could ease some of the burden on time.

2. **Protect your "magic time."**

In his book *The Perfect Day Formula*, Chris Ballantyne defines your "magic time" as the time of the day where you can get three times as much work done as you would at any other time of day. You probably already know when that time is for you. As a self-described morning person, when I was in college, I never pulled an all-nighter. Rather than willing myself awake with caffeine, when I had an exam or big paper due, I'd go to sleep by 10 p.m. and wake up at 4 a.m. to work with a fresh mind.

Clearly, my magic time has always been first thing in the morning. Whatever that time is for you, do your best to protect it – and then use it for actual focused work time. When I was in a corporate job that meant blocking off three mornings a week to work and scheduling meetings around that time. Of course, there were times when I had to make exceptions (even multiple times a week), but there was no doubt that I was able to protect more of my time by being proactive rather than reactive with my calendar.

3. **Decrease distractions.**

Research shows that it takes anywhere from 11-25 minutes to return to a task after being interrupted. It's no wonder we can be busy all day and yet get nothing done. I have found that, in addition to blocking off time to work, minimizing distractions helps me get more done in less time.

This could mean a lot of things for you – such as turning off the Outlook email pop up notification on your computer, only checking emails at specific times (e.g. first thing, before lunch, and before you leave for the day), and turning your phone face-side down or even setting it on airplane mode so you don't see all the updates. If you work in an open office and coworkers often just stop by with questions or to chat, you might see if there is somewhere else you can go to work. When I experienced this issue, I found that bringing my laptop to a conference room or the cafeteria was a great way to seize some focused, non-interrupted time.

4. **Batch your tasks.**

Similarly to the way that interruptions can make it hard to get back to the task at hand, changing back and forth between very different activities can make it harder to get in the zone of productivity. This is where batching – scheduling like activities together – comes in. You probably already do this in your personal life when you make a list of all the errands you are going to run on Saturday morning, or set aside a couple hours to do all the cleaning at home. Depending on your type of work, this could mean scheduling a couple hours or even an entire day of similar tasks, such as writing, calls, administrative duties, and so on.

5. **Take breaks.**

I've read that the average attention span of Americans is eight seconds, less than that of a goldfish. Yet we're expected to sit at a desk and work for eight, ten, twelve hours straight. While taking a break every few seconds might not be feasible, studies show that getting up to stretch or take a quick walk every 50-90 minutes actually helps productivity. Set a timer and experiment with it and see what works for you. I have found that just knowing that a break is coming up gives me motivation to stay focused and get more done.

Manage Your Mindset

Setting boundaries and improving your productivity are great tools for feeling more empowered and happy at work. Something a little less obvious, but just as – if not more – important is mindset. When you're unhappy, it's natural to focus on the bad. But I am going to challenge you to seek out – and focus on – the good. I'm not asking you to turn a blind eye to all that is wrong. But after acknowledging it, I want you to find reasons to be grateful for your current job.

Take Joe, an IT manager at a small company who acknowledges that he was frustrated with management, empty promises of promotions, and work overload. The silver lining in these issues though, is that they are teaching him to stand up for himself and to set boundaries. Beyond the challenges, he also appreciates that he is able to work on a variety of projects and is always learning. He also has the flexibility in hours to come in and leave early on Fridays when he has to pick his kids up from school.

Kacey used to complain that her part-time job at a call center was mind numbing and that her boss was a micromanager. But after spending some time looking at the good – that she got insurance for herself and her family without having to work full-time and had afternoons free to be with her kids – she realized that the meaning in her job was not the work itself, but how it allowed her to care for her family outside of work.

While both very different, Joe and Kacey demonstrate how simply being grateful can make a difference. Finding the good does not mean that you won't work to make things better, or even look for another job. But it does help to shift your perspective and get you out of your head when you are frustrated at work.

Although complaining can feel cathartic in the moment, it only attracts more of that negativity and, more often than not, puts you in a bad mood. Decide now that you will focus on the good – even write down a gratitude list or keep one in your phone to look over during particularly tough times. The next few chapters are dedicated to helping you find a new job, but while you are at this job, remind yourself that you always have a choice to stay or leave. This alone can be very empowering.

You might say, "Oh, well I don't have a choice. I need the money," but that is a choice, too. No one is pulling you out of bed and forcing you to go to work each day. In this example, you're deciding to keep a job you don't like because the paycheck is more important than how you feel about your work. And that's a perfectly fine choice, which you can change at any time. Just knowing that you are taking steps (like reading this book!) to turn your situation around instantly converts you from helpless victim to empowered self-starter.

Actively Seek Joy

You have more control over your happiness than I bet you realize – 40 percent to be exact. Researchers have found that while half of our state of mind is determined by genetics and 10 percent is determined by events outside our control, the rest comes from a conscious effort to be happy. Simply put – if you want more joy at work and in your life, actively seek it out.

Get creative. How can you find the bigger purpose in your work right now? If it's not the actual work specific to your role, maybe it's being part of a project that's important and that's making a difference. Or maybe it's the coaching and mentoring of the people you work with that provides meaning and fulfillment for you.

Consider how you could make working more enjoyable. If you are bored and in need of a challenge, keep your eyes open for opportunities to join a team that is solving a new problem or working on a new initiative. Think about ways you can fix problems in your own area, such as streamlining a process, setting up a new template, or automating tasks. Determine what you want to learn to either make you better at your current job, or set you up for the next one, and go learn it – whether or not on your employer's watch or dime. All of this can go a long way in making you feel productive, accomplished, and in line with your professional goals.

Maybe you have the opposite problem, and as mentioned in the boundaries section, you need to have a conversation with your manager about workload and priorities – and then make sure to take lunch and leave on time.

In addition, perhaps you could look into asking for flexible hours. A lot of companies will let you work longer days Monday through Thursday, and then give you Friday off. I found that for me, a work-from-home day a couple times a month would do wonders for my sanity, productivity, and happiness (plus nothing beats working in yoga pants).

Even brightening up your workspace with things that make you feel good can make a big difference. That could translate into bringing in fresh flowers, or placing a picture of people you love, or something that reminds you of your "why," in your line of sight. I like to have healthy snacks, a grounding essential oil, and my favorite hand cream close by – anything to lift my mood. I am also big on inspirational quotes and always have at least one or two up to help me stay positive.

Here is a picture of a quote on a mini-easel I kept at my desk years ago, reminding me to not get so caught up in the day-to-day that I forgot the bigger picture. Check out Danielle LaPorte's truthbomb decks for more inspiration.

Now let's look outside the four walls of your office. What can you do outside of work to bring more meaning and happiness to your life right now? Many of us who are very successful have gotten to this place by sacrificing other areas of life like relationships, health, and fun. We put off those things that bring us joy for a later time, when we are successful enough, far along enough in our career to relax.

Think about what you've been putting off and make a decision to start doing some of those things. Can you spend more time with friends? Sign up for a workshop that lets you be creative, like a paint and wine or pottery class? Volunteer, take a trapeze class, go to a show, get a manicure, read a book, or watch Disney movies – anything that will let you unwind, laugh, and take your mind off work.

Do you see how it's all connected? If you have a more full life, and plans after work, then you're going to have to stick to the boundaries you set. And because you're leaving at a certain time, you'll naturally be more productive. All of this is good for you, and good for your work.

Will it take effort? Yes. Will it feel uncomfortable? Absolutely. But when you realize that not only are you creating a healthier, happier, and more meaningful day for yourself, but that you are a better employee as well, this way of working will become non-negotiable. That, my friend, is the secret to having a kick-ass productive day and still making it to 6 p.m. spin class.

Now that we've talked about how to survive and be happy now, the next step is figuring out what you're going to do. Are you going to stay? Look for a new job? Explore an entirely new career? Turn to the next chapter to explore your options.

JOY NOTES

- Set boundaries to protect your time, health, and overall well-being.
- Take care of yourself. Get enough sleep, move your body and eat quality food.
- Be more productive at work by minimizing meetings, protecting your time, decreasing distractions, batching tasks, and taking breaks.

- Manage your mindset. Focus on the positive and remember that you always have a choice.
- You are in control of your experience. Actively seek out joy – both at, and outside of, work.

CHAPTER FOUR

Should I Stay or Should I Go?
Deciding Your Next Steps

You have brains in your head. You have feet in your
shoes. You can steer yourself any direction you choose.
~ DR. SEUSS

"Stuck" is a common feeling for those of us that are unhappy and unfulfilled at work. It is natural to feel paralyzed because either we think we have no option but to stay, or the opposite – there seem to be so many options that it becomes overwhelming and so we do nothing.

Should you stay or should you go? It's as simple as that, at least to start with. My guess is that if you picked up this book, you already know the answer in your heart – and it's not to stay. If that's the case, feel free to jump ahead to the next chapter. If you're not sure, it's time to get out your journal or open up a fresh Word doc and answer the following eight questions. You started to explore these in Chapter 2, but now it's time to get more specific.

1. Is this a healthy work environment for me? This includes:
    - physical workspace
    - culture, politics
    - leadership and team dynamic
    - feelings when at work or thinking about work (accomplishment, satisfaction, camaraderie v. stress, frustration, dread)
2. Do I enjoy my work? Could I enjoy it under the right circumstances?
3. Do I like the people I work with? Do I respect my boss?
4. Is there room for career advancement through either promotion or lateral moves?
5. Does my work feel meaningful to me? Am I proud of my work I do and the company that employs me?
6. Am I (can I be) successful here?
7. Am I happy at this job?
8. Does this job allow me the time and resources to focus on my stated non-work priorities (e.g. relationships, family, health, travel, fun)?

If you've answered yes to all the questions above – congratulations! You have an awesome job and career! Put this book down and enjoy it!

If you answered no to any, or multiple, questions above – the next step is to ask yourself if it's possible for your answer to change at your current job. For example, if you don't like your work, could a conversation about responsibilities with your manager help? Or could you delegate some of your less enjoyable, but time-consuming tasks, and focus more on the work you do love? How about volunteering for projects that are more enjoyable and meaningful to you?

Elizabeth and I started working together after the market research firm she worked for went through two layoffs in a period of just six months. She was worried about losing her job, and on top of that, was now doing the work of three people. Stressed, unhappy, tired, and discouraged about the prospect of ever getting promoted there, it was clear she had to make a change. But Elizabeth wasn't sure what she wanted to do or what her options were. Plus, it had been nearly a decade since she looked for a job, so the thought of that was actually just as scary to her as staying.

Over the period of a couple months, Elizabeth got clear on what she wanted from her career and what her current job was costing her. While she liked the work, for the sake of her well-being, she could no longer stay in that toxic environment. After looking at other market research firms and deciding they wouldn't be much better, she chose to work with a consulting firm to do freelance market research for nearby companies. It was a similar job but with more freedom, exposure to new companies, people, and ways of working. After a year of freelancing, Elizabeth chose to work for one of her clients, but in an entirely new role on a product development team.

If, like Elizabeth, you are clear that there is no way to change your situation at your current job, the next logical step is to think about leaving. You've got two options here – either you can look for a similar job in your industry or completely change careers. If you generally like your work and believe you could be fulfilled, if not for all the issues at your current company, then finding a new job could be your next step. But if you know that this is not the work for you, and that no matter how wonderful the people, the culture, and the benefits of a company are, you would not be fulfilled, then it's time to consider another career.

It's sounds so simple on paper, but it can be crazy scary to realize that you need to make a move. In 12-step programs, one of the first and most difficult things you have to do is admit you have a problem. It's no different here. Being honest with yourself, and then making the decision to change, is the first step in an exciting, and no-doubt scary, journey to having a job and career you love.

This would be a good time to refer back to the questions you answered in Chapter 2 regarding what this job is costing you and your new definition of success. How do your answers align with your current situation? (If you skimmed that chapter, go back now and spend some time on those exercises. Clarity in this area is so important before you decide to make any big changes.)

Many times when I've felt on the edge of a life-changing decision, I just wish someone would tell me what to do. That some all-knowing, omnipresent force could tell me the right choice or action so that I would be guaranteed success and happiness.

We all know that unfortunately, that won't happen – and that the answer is inside us. That only we know what is best for us. But what if you can't hear your own inner wisdom over the cacophony of worry and fear inside your head? For that, I've got a small but powerful trick – ask yourself this bonus question:

What would your older, wiser, more experienced,
future self say?

Really. I want you to imagine yourself 20 years from now. What would that person tell you to do? Would she tell you to stick it out a little longer? Or would she say that you've wasted enough time and encourage you to explore other options? Would she tell you to quit now? Or stay in this job while you explore other "less practical" passions? Maybe she'd urge you to look into starting your own business?

After you've asked your future self this question, get quiet and listen. Often the answer will come right away. If not, journaling or meditation can help – or even just throwing the question out there and trusting that the answer will come to you. I can't quite explain the magic of taking advice from your future self, but there's something about changing perspectives in this way that can help you get our of your head and look at the situation from an unbiased, unemotional, and long-term point of view. Give it a try; you've got nothing to lose.

After you've gained some clarity around what next steps are right for you (or even while you are working through it), read on for tools and strategies to build your exit plan while dealing with and minimizing uncertainty – whether that means changing jobs or even careers.

JOY NOTES

- You don't have to stay stuck. No matter what, you always have options.
- If you are not satisfied with, and cannot change your current work situation, consider looking for a new job.
- If the problems in your current role would be the same no matter your employer, consider changing careers.
- When you're not sure what to do, ask your future self for advice.

PART 3

Act

What you seek is seeking you.

~ RUMI

CHAPTER FIVE

Takin' Care of Business
Finding a New Job

Every new beginning comes from some other beginning's end.

~ SEMISONIC, "CLOSING TIME"

So you've decided to look for a new job. Instead of referring to it as a job search, I like to call it job attraction. That simple word change is a reminder that you are drawing in the perfect job for you, not just searching for any ol' job.

Whether you're looking for the same job at a different company or looking to completely change careers, this chapter is the place to start. For those changing careers, the next chapter will have additional information on how to bridge the gap between your new career and your experience thus far. Either way, if you choose to leave your current position, you must do so with the intention of landing in a place where your work will bring you the meaning and happiness that you are now lacking. Otherwise, it's just another job with a different set of problems.

My aim for these chapters is to provide a strategy plus tangible action items to help you land the job you desire. What you will *not* find in the following pages are job search 101 topics like how to build your résumé or prep for interviews. If you need help with those, there are a plethora of books and articles dedicated solely to those topics.

I am sometimes asked about working with recruiters. I think it's one tool in your job attraction strategy, but not one I would rely on. Remember, recruiters work for companies, not you. Helping you land your desired dream job is understandably not their priority. Simply put, if you've worked with, and had success with recruiters in the past, I would continue to engage them, but be sure not to invest a substantial amount of your time there.

Before we jump into strategy, a quick note for those seeking new employment while maintaining their current job: Do not use company property, time, or resources to conduct your job search. Not only would you not want your boss to find your résumé on the printer, but it's also out of integrity to look for a job on your employer's time, as you are still getting paid to work there. You can get creative – I've even had clients take their personal computer or a tablet to work so that they could check emails and job postings at Starbucks on their lunch breaks – but make sure to focus on your work while you're at work.

There are three steps to attracting the job of your dreams. You must have:

1. A Clear Message,
2. Aligned Personal Brand, and
3. Smart Promotion.

Sounds like a marketing campaign, right? That's because looking for a job is just that, except *you* are the product and service. Take department stores, for example. Essentially, they're all the same, right? Nope. Macy's and Saks Fifth Avenue are both big box stores that sell everything from cosmetics to clothes, but the thought of each conjures up a completely different image. That's because their messaging, branding, and promotion are different.

Macy's has historically been known for mid-level brands and many sales, and appeals to a wide range of demographics and income levels. It is fancier than a Kohls, but more approachable than say, Nordstrom. Now think of Saks Fifth Avenue, also a department store, but one that most of us would consider high-end. Its customers skew higher income and prefer luxury brands. Even the look and feel of the inside of the store is decidedly opulent when directly compared to Macy's.

We know all this because of a combination of these stores' messaging, branding, and promotion. Everything from their taglines, to their ads, to their online presence and in-store experience add up to create a reputation and personal opinion about the store. When all three are aligned, we as consumers know who they are and if they are a fit for our needs.

What works for products and services also works for people. Imagine Bill Gates and Steve Jobs, both pioneers in the computer industry. Think of Tony Robbins and Oprah, both huge contributors to the self-help industries and proponents of becoming the best version of yourself. Consider Barack Obama and Donald Trump, both presidents of the United States. These people all do, or have done, similar work – yet they are completely different due to what they stand for, who they appeal to, and how they promote themselves. And the same holds true for you and your job search (attraction).

Clear Message

The first step in looking for a new job is getting clear on your messaging. That starts with the knowledge of who you are and what you offer in the context of your desired job. The next step is determining your target audience, and then clearly articulating your message to those people.

If you've been following along with the questions in this book so far, you should be clear about what you want in your next job. Next, I want you to write out both what you want in a job (include non-negotiables) and a list of the top ten companies you'd like to work for. This will help you be laser focused in your search and say no to opportunities that might be tempting, but will ultimately not lead to the happiness and fulfillment you are seeking.

Carlo, an IT consultant who lives in a suburb of Chicago, knew it was time to make a move when, despite stellar client reviews and three years of management promises, he was again passed over for a promotion. He enjoyed his job but realized that there was no room for advancement at his current firm. One of the first things I asked him to do was write down a list of everything he wanted in his new job. In addition to an exhaustive list of the firms he wanted to work for, he listed the following five non-negotiables:

- Location: Chicago area or ability to work remotely
- Salary: $75-110K total compensation, depending on size of firm
- Level: Senior Manager or higher, depending on firm
- Travel: no more than 25 percent
- Opportunity to manage a team and build leadership skills

It may have taken a little longer than if he just settled for the first offer that came his way, but by recognizing his needs and sticking to them, Carlo landed a job at a higher level and with more pay than he anticipated.

After getting clear on your target job and companies, you need to be able to articulate what you offer, or your benefits. In other words, how do your years and type of experience, formal and informal education, and passion both inside and outside of work – make you the perfect person for said job?

Next is your "why" statement, or what is commonly referred to as your "elevator pitch." Whether at a networking event, on a flight, or literally in an elevator, it is so important to be able to communicate your message clearly and succinctly.

If you've ever found yourself stumbling over your words when someone asked you what you do, then you'll appreciate this even more. Having a few lines memorized will make it easier to clearly articulate who you are, the value you bring, and what you are looking for, before losing someone's attention. Then as the conversation continues, you can get into more of the details.

There are many ways to pull together an elevator pitch, but I like to use the following formula:

Why Statement = Your Name

+

Who (you help)

+

How (you help them)

+

Where (you are looking to do this work)

Here is an example from Austin who had worked in consulting for five years after college and wanted to move into industry. "I love helping companies improve their customer experience. I do this by uncovering and fixing operational inefficiencies that affect the online customer journey including ease of checkout and usefulness of auto-generated recommendations. In my consulting career, I've worked with over ten of the retail industry's top brands. I am now looking to do this work at one retailer so that I can make even more of an impact."

Aligned Personal Brand

After you are clear on your message, the next step is to build (or refine) your personal brand so that it is aligned with your why statement and will resonate with your target audience. One of the first articles on personal branding was published in Fast Company over 20 years ago. In "The Brand Called You," Tom Peters told readers, *"We are CEOs of our own companies: Me Inc. To be in business today, our most important job is to be head marketer for the brand called You."* He believed that your personal brand was your ticket to differentiating yourself and to creating and landing a role perfect for you. I couldn't agree more.

Your personal brand incorporates your talents, accomplishments, and what you stand for (or want to stand for). Just as is true for Macy's, Oprah, or any product or celebrity, your personal brand is defined by your reputation – by what people think of when they hear your name. It is how you are perceived in person and online, and can play a significant role in whether you land the job or don't even get an interview. The good news is that you have a lot of control over it.

Let's cover in-person first. Professionally, this would include how you are known around the office, and if applicable, in your industry. It is how you show up at networking events and even in personal situations that may include your professional contacts. Think about the skills that you are always complimented on, and if you have become a go-to person for particular types of projects. Is this what you want to be known for? If not, think of ways you can make changes to make your reputation more aligned with your goals. Say you work in an office as a marketing manager and are known for making the best brownies and organizing great celebrations. That may be fine if you're an aspiring baker or event planner, but if you want to be known for your marketing prowess, you may need to keep the baked goods at home and speak up at the next meeting, perhaps even volunteer to present at it.

Just as important as your in-person reputation, is your online presence. That's because it's often your first impression – it's how people judge you before they even get to meet you, or before they know you well. We all do this. Whether we're meeting a new colleague at a business lunch or a considering a potential date with someone we met on a dating app, the first thing most of us do is google them. If your online presence is on-point and aligned with your goals and your message, you make it easy for hiring managers to see that you are right for a job before they've even heard your voice. But if it's not, you'll never know how many opportunities you've missed out on because someone made a judgment of you based on what they found online. Below are four areas in which to manage your online presence to help you meet your job attraction goals.

1. **Audit your online presence regularly.**

    Start with a general Google search to make sure nothing comes up that you wouldn't want a recruiter or prospective employer seeing. If something does, do what you can to take it down, untag yourself, or ask the website owner to do the same.

    On the flip side of the coin, make sure that *something* comes up, even if it is just your LinkedIn account. Believe it or not, in today's world, having zero presence can be just as much of a red flag as having a negative one. You might just be a private person or have never needed a LinkedIn account because you've been with the same firm since graduating college. But people will wonder why you don't have it and may assume that you have something to hide or aren't tech savvy – neither of which is helpful for someone looking for a new job.

Keep on top of your online presence by periodically searching your name, setting up a Google alert, or even using an online reputation service like BrandYourself to alert you of any potentially negative search results.

2. **Review non-professional social media accounts.**
   If a potential hiring manager saw your Facebook, Instagram, Snapchat, and Pinterest boards, would it help or hurt you? Especially if it's the latter, but even if it's neutral, think about making it private and/or deleting any posts or comments that are not doing you any favors. Going forward, before you post, comment, or share, consider if it is adding value and aligned with your personal brand. Negativity, politics, and anything polarizing are generally all hot buttons to avoid – unless of course that is part of your brand and will help you get the job.

3. **Update your LinkedIn profile.**
   So as to not tip off your current employer, before you do make any updates, make sure to turn off notifications

for activity and profile changes. Then go ahead and update your profile with the following:

- **Recent and professional headshot**: This goes without saying, but no selfies or pictures from ten years (and 30 pounds!) ago. Remember, this could be your first impression; it is worth investing in professional pictures.

- **Headline**: LinkedIn will auto populate this with your title, but I recommend putting your top skills in your headline to help communicate your message and the skills that most apply to the job you are seeking, all before anyone even clicks on your profile. So rather than "social media manager," you might write "digital marketing expert, social media influencer, SEO."

- **Experience and Skills**: Beyond just updating your experience, be sure to include accomplishments, awards, and articles you may have written. Similar to résumé bullet points, start each line with a verb and use numbers whenever possible (e.g. manage a team of ten people, cut costs by 20 percent, closed 80 percent of deals). Think about what key words are most common in the job descriptions you are looking at and include them in both the experience and skills sections of your profile. Finally, if past experience, certifications, etc. do not directly or indirectly show how you'd be a fit for your current dream job, consider deleting them altogether as to not distract from the message, skills, and experience that do.

- **Recommendations**: While it's best to get into the habit of asking people for a recommendation after a successful project or big win, it's not too late to add a review or two to your profile. Since it could tip your boss off, it might not be wise to ask her for a recommendation, but how about a client or someone you worked with at a previous engagement? Even words of praise from a volunteer coordinator can be helpful in building up your profile and providing additional social proof as to what a great person you are.

- **Opportunities setting**: Another relatively new feature is in the privacy section, where you now have the ability to turn on the option to signal to recruiters and hiring managers that you're open to new positions. It is not public; your coworkers and manager will not be able to see it (except in the rare case that they are hiring managers and happen to be looking at your profile).

4. **Secure a personal website.**

   If available, buy your own domain name. You might not need it today – if that's the case, just forward it to your LinkedIn account – but you'll be happy you have it in a few years when you do. And even if that day never comes, it's one more way to control what comes up in searches of your name, and ensure that someone with the same name, and with a lesser reputation, doesn't negatively affect you.

Smart Promotion

For products and services, promotion includes everything from TV, online, and print advertising to in-store sales and customer experience. For you, it will mainly be about networking, supported by your online presence. Armed with clarity around what you are seeking, a clear message that communicates your value, and an understanding of target audience (companies), it's time to start talking to people. I know – networking gets a bad rap. But consider the fact that multiple studies have shown that nearly 85 percent of all jobs are filled via networking. This has been true for both my clients and myself, with literally all my post-college jobs coming from referrals.

The first step to successful promotion is getting in front of your target audience. Just as a health food brand might advertise at a gym or in a fitness magazine, you need to be where your people – colleagues, hiring managers, and recruiters in your industry and at your preferred companies – are. Look into conferences, networking groups, and associations to start with, and learn to see any social event as an opportunity to practice delivering your message. You never know who you'll meet in line at Starbucks, at the gym, or while making your way through airport security.

When we get to the promotion stage, many clients tell me that – for a variety of reasons from shyness to a discomfort with self-promotion – the thought of networking makes them cringe. But as mentioned above, it is an absolutely necessary step in finding your next job. To that end, here are my top five networking tips.

1. **Make friends.**

   We've talked about it before, and I'll say it again. Mindset is so important. Reframe your current notion of networking to include the idea of meeting and connecting with like-minded people. It's not about one event, but about building mutually beneficial relationships over the long term.

2. **Only attend events that excite you.**

   If you don't want to be somewhere, it will likely show in your energy and affect your interactions, defeating the whole purpose of going. Find events that are actually of interest to you so that you get something out of it even if you don't make any great contacts (friends).

3. **Be present and hit your quota.**

   Especially for introverts, the idea of talking to a bunch of strangers can be daunting. So set a quota. Tell yourself you'll go to one networking event a week or that at each one, you can leave when you've talked to three people. Many times, you'll want to stay longer, but if not, there's no guilt.

   As with most things in life, when it comes to networking, I believe in quality over quantity. You'll get more value and make more friends by engaging in just a few genuine conversations rather than working the room and leaving with the most business cards at the end of the night. Knowing that your goal is quality over quantity will also allow you to be present and have more meaningful conversations. You don't want to be the person that's half listening and looking over someone's shoulder for the next person to talk to.

4. Add value.

One of the reasons networking can be so uncomfortable is because we think the only purpose is to get something from someone. So don't do that. Whether making an introduction or simply recommending a book, look to add value and let the relationship develop naturally before asking for anything. Many times, you won't even have to ask because as people get to know you, they'll naturally think of you for opportunities that are a fit.

5. Arrive on time and leave early.

I used to think that showing up fashionably late was the best strategy for networking events, but realized that this can actually make it harder to break into conversations as groups have already formed. If you show up on time, you'll be with a smaller, less intimidating group and thus, more likely to be approached.

Then give yourself the luxury of leaving early. As Susan Cain says in her book *Quiet: The Power of Introverts in a World That Can't Stop Talking*, "Introverts... may have strong social skills and enjoy parties and business meetings, but after a while wish they were home in their pajamas." Is this you? If so, just knowing that you don't have to stay the whole time can be enough motivation to actually get to an event. Decide before you go that you can leave whenever you've hit your limit. Most people won't even notice you've left, and those that do will just be happy that you were there in the first place.

In addition to in-person networking, use online networking not just to connect with the people you meet, but also make new connections, especially at the companies you'd like to work for. On LinkedIn, rather than just requesting to connect, customize your invite with a couple sentences to introduce yourself and your reason for connecting. You might, for example, say that you were impressed by their background (assuming you were) and would love to connect and learn more about their experience. If and when they connect, follow up and suggest a few times to talk. If 10-20 percent of the people you reach out to result in a conversation, consider yourself lucky.

When you do talk, even if you don't use the words "informational interview," treat it like one. Come prepared with questions (don't just say you want to "pick their brain"), respect their time, and thank them for speaking with you. In order to stay top of mind, it's okay to follow up every month or two as long as you're adding value such as sharing an article or letting them know about an event they might be interested in.

Although not to be relied on, you can also use LinkedIn to learn about and apply for jobs online. This probably won't be how you get your job, but it can be leveraged as a form of research to refine your message and update your résumé and LinkedIn profile to better fit the jobs you are seeking.

A clear message, aligned personal brand, and smart promotion will help you attract the job of your dreams. If you know that you need to leave your current job, but believe that the barriers to achieving your new definition of success are just too high in this career or industry, then it's time to consider a career change. If that's what you choose to do, the above-mentioned steps still hold true, but you'll need to do more work to bridge the gap between your current and your new career.

JOY NOTES

- When looking for a new job, think of yourself as the product.
- A clear message, aligned personal brand and smart promotion are the keys to job attraction success.
- Your online presence should reflect your skills, experience and education that make you a perfect fit for your dream job.
- Networking is necessary, but doesn't have to be a drag. Make friends, add value, and leave early to make the most of your social time.

CHAPTER SIX

Runnin' Down a Dream
Building a New Career

It's never too late to be what you might have been.
~ GEORGE ELIOT

Although I've seen inconsistent statistics on the number of times people change careers throughout their lifetime, I think we can all agree that gone are the days of working for one company from college graduation to retirement, in exchange for a gold watch and a healthy pension. No doubt, the idea of changing careers can seem scary, if not impossible, but if you're reading this, I suspect that the thought of living out the rest of your years in your current career is even scarier. The way I look at it, you have nothing to lose. It never hurts to do some research and explore your options; and if you decide against changing careers, you can always stay (or go back) to exactly where you are now.

71

When compared to a traditional job search, changing careers will require more planning and action necessary to make your dream a reality. Using the last chapter's steps as our foundation, and adding one additional step, we'll build your career change plan below.

Clear Message

When changing careers, it is more important than ever to spend the time to get clear on exactly what it is you want to do – and as you learn more, to continually refine your desires and corresponding message. You might already have an idea of what you want to do. If not, in addition to the questions in the last chapter, here are a few more general ones to consider:

- What do you enjoy doing in your free time now?
- What problems do you like to solve?
- Who do you want to serve?
- What would you do if you could do anything?
- What were your passions as a kid?
- What do you get complimented on all the time?

As with the other big questions in this book, it makes sense to dedicate a notebook or Word document plus a good amount of time to exploring these questions. It is likely that the answer is right under your nose, and something you're so good at, you take for granted.

Andrea, a former client and now good friend of mine, used to have a job in marketing for a healthcare company. For years, she had been asked to speak at industry conferences. It was something she enjoyed doing, plus it allowed her to get out of the office and go to events that would otherwise not be within budget.

Because speaking came easy to her, she didn't realize how special her gift was. While most people would request to pay to speak at a conference – she was not only sought after, but had her travel and accommodations compensated for – all for a 20-minute talk. It wasn't until we spent some time with the above questions that it became clear she should give serious thought to making a career out of speaking. Just a couple years after leaving her corporate job, Andrea now makes a living through freelance healthcare consulting and you guessed it – speaking – at industry events.

While she technically changed careers, it doesn't feel like a far stretch from the work she was doing before. By leveraging her healthcare expertise and passion for speaking, Andrea was able to create a job that she loves.

Once you have at least a general idea of what you want to do next, it's your goal to bridge the gap between your current experience and what's needed for the job you want. This is just like how we built the message in the previous chapter, but will require a little more thought and creativity to show how your skills and background actually make you the perfect fit for this new job.

I'll use myself as an example here – this is how this process worked for me. When I first knew I was ready to leave consulting, I wasn't sure what I wanted to do next, except that it had to be a role at one company and allow me to do work I enjoyed. So I then looked at the work I had been doing for the last several years and decided to look for a job that included the "good" stuff – strategy, big idea thinking, finding and communicating solutions – but that did not involve my least favorite tasks, such as spending the entire day in Excel. I wanted my own team and more leeway to be creative and manage projects my way. Through conversations and research, I would later found out that this is the description of a Strategy Director.

Then I looked at industries I'd be interested in. I have always loved psychology and marketing, so retail, an industry built on understanding and selling to people seemed like a great fit. Finally, I wrote down a list of the top ten companies I would like to work for and got to researching them and making connections with people who worked there. As I talked to more and more people, I gained more clarity about the job I wanted, and refined my message accordingly. When building my elevator pitch and sharing my story, I focused on the skills and experience that applied to the new role and took note of what they thought I was missing – so that I could either get the experience or figure out how to address their concern.

Aligned Personal Brand

In addition to the personal branding strategies in the previous chapter, there are ways you can leverage your online presence to showcase yourself as an expert – or at the very least, an involved part of your desired industry or career. I did this by adding value to my networks by sharing and commenting on relevant retail strategy articles on LinkedIn and Twitter and even writing blog posts about retail events I attended. The effort to do this was minimal since I already had a daily reading routine (see additional step below), but it positioned me as someone who was part of the conversation – and gave me a connection to the retail industry in online searches. It was also responsible for at least a handful of valuable connections that even led to interviews.

Consider how this could work for you. It could be as simple as sharing articles like I did, posting your involvement at industry events, or even just showcasing your relevant skills in a more obvious way on your LinkedIn profile.

Smart Promotion

When it comes to promotion, or networking, the essentials are the same. The only difference is that you will likely need to be a little more proactive since your network is less likely to include a plethora of contacts in your desired career and industry.

I recommend initially focusing your efforts on getting informational interviews (mentioned in the previous chapter), as they will help you not only make contacts but also serve as research and help you get clearer on your message. This is not just about making connections, but about learning more about your desired job and career change. Think about what you need to know to be successful in your search, and as you get answers to those questions, adjust for each person. In general it makes sense to start high level and then get into the specifics of their experience and current role. Here are a few questions to get you started:

- How did you get into this industry? (interests, experience, education)
- What do you like most/least about the industry? Role? Company?
- What do you look for when hiring someone for this role?
- If you were in my position, what would be your next steps?
- Any other advice?
- Is there anyone else you can connect me with as I gather information?

Aim to reach out to and request informational interviews from five people in your desired field each week, with the goal of talking to at least four new contacts each month. In addition to informational interviews, join and get involved with relevant LinkedIn groups, industry organizations and in-person events as a way to both learn and meet new people.

Additional Step – Get Smart

Whether you're changing industries or jobs, or both, you need to get smart – fast – about this new world. This will help you refine your messaging – what you want and what you offer – as well as your expectations. It will also aid in building your personal brand so that your résumé, LinkedIn profile, and online presence support your ability to transition into this new career. In addition, being up to speed on the latest in your new desired field will make for easier conversations as you network. Having an understanding of the problems could also shed light on new ways that you can add value. In short, if you want to change careers, you should be living and breathing your desired world. Here are four ways to do just that:

1. **Create a reading routine.**

   As you talk to people in the industry or field you are looking to transition into, ask them what their favorite books, news sources, and newsletters are. Then buy (and read!) the books and subscribe to get email updates. The first 15 minutes of your day should be spent reading the news to understand events, companies, trends, and key players in this new world. This will make networking a lot easier as you'll have common ground to start with. Something as simple as being up on industry news can make it feel to them as though you're already "one of them," as opposed to an outsider trying to break in.

2. **Do your research.**

   You will also need to do some deep research – on the industry, target companies, and the jobs you are interested in. View profiles and talk to people who already have the role you want to determine if additional certifications or degrees are required. When you meet new people in person, or reach out online, request an informational interview to learn more about their role, company, and industry. For some, this makes it easier to network because now they have an "excuse" for a conversation, while also creating connections and relationships for the long-term.

3. **Get educated.**

   Depending on the change you are looking to make, you may need to learn more than what you can read in books and online. Nowadays, with the democratization of education, there are many free online courses you can take. It started with the likes of Udemy and Coursera, and now you can even take free courses on a wide range of topics from Harvard, MIT, and Berkeley. Online resources are great, just be sure not to use them in place of in-person events, as attending conferences, luncheons, and panel discussions can serve the dual purposes of education and networking.

4. **Gain relevant experience.**

   Get creative and find ways to get exposed to the type of work you want to do. This could be as simple as showing interest and signing up for a project in another department at work. There may also be ways you can volunteer to get the experience. Say you're looking to move from marketing to finance – you could raise your hand to do the bookkeeping at your church or favorite charity. Or you could look into getting involved with an organization like Taproot, specifically set up to connect professionals willing to volunteer their time with companies that need their skills.

While it will take more effort and time to switch careers than to just change jobs, it is absolutely doable and worth it to find the meaning and happiness you are missing now. I know, because I've been there and made it to the other side. I almost didn't do it because I was afraid that with nearly a decade in consulting, no company would give me a chance, and if they did, I'd have to start at the bottom. It didn't help that some well-meaning friends confirmed this belief, because they had the same fears (and because of that, had resigned themselves to staying in a job that made them miserable and sick). But I am telling you, it simply isn't true – and I have seen that, not only for myself, but for my clients as well.

Whenever we make a big change, challenges are sure to arise. In the next chapter, we'll look at the top obstacles to finding a new job or building a new career, and how to overcome them.

JOY NOTES

- No matter your background, you can always change careers. You have nothing to lose by exploring something new. And if you make a change and don't like it, you can always return to your current career.
- It is your responsibility to bridge the gap between your current role and the job you want. Do this by highlighting relevant skills and projects, and gaining applicable experience when necessary.
- Use informational interviews as a tool to learn more, refine your message, and meet people in your desired industry.

- Make a concerted effort to learn more about your desired role and industry through a regular reading routine, online and in-person research, additional education and seeking out relevant experience.

CHAPTER SEVEN

I Will Survive
Overcoming Your Fears

And the day came when the risk to remain tight in a
bud was more painful than the risk it took to blossom.
~ ANAIS NIN

A s with any big change and new undertaking, you can expect to hit challenges along the way – doubts and fears, both real and imagined, that can stall you and possibly even prevent you from starting. Below you'll find the top fears that my clients and I have encountered and the solutions we used to conquer them.

Fear #1: I don't have enough time.

This is probably the most common, and understandable, reason we put off getting anything done – from losing weight, to learning a new language, to writing that book. I get it.

You're working a full-time job and barely have enough time to juggle all your other responsibilities. The truth is that there will never be a perfect time, and that if it is important enough, you'll find a way. But you don't have to make it so hard.

Solution: Commit to 30 minutes a day, most days.

While it's true that you *can* make looking for a job a full-time job, it doesn't have to be this way. In fact, you can be just as, if not more, effective when you follow a targeted plan. To avoid becoming overwhelmed with the larger task of finding a job, break your goal into smaller, more distinct action steps. Commit to doing just a little each day, and working it into your schedule so that it becomes part of your routine, just like brushing your teeth. At the beginning, you may have to schedule it like you would a meeting or time at the gym. Here are a few examples of activities mentioned in previous chapters, that when broken down into daily or weekly tasks, don't take a lot of time but support your desire to find a new job.

- **Create a 15-minute reading ritual each weekday morning**.

  As discussed in a previous chapter, whether you're changing careers or seeking the same job at a similar company, it's always a good idea to be up on the latest in your field. Subscribe to a few newsletters or bookmark your favorite industry websites and spend the first 15 minutes of your day reading up on the news and the trends relevant to your industry and career. This will help you with networking conversations, allow you to add value by sharing relevant articles, and possibly even spark new ideas for your overall job search.

- **Reach out to five contacts per day**.
  Depending on your situation, this could be cold emailing on LinkedIn or following up and maintaining relationships with your current contacts. Say you're seeking a new career and your goal is to reach out to five new contacts per day. It won't take that long, but even if you only do this five days a week, you've got 100 people that you've reached out to over the course of a month. Assuming a conservative 10 to 20 percent response rate, that's 10 to 20 brand new contacts in a month that have the potential to lead to your next opportunity. This is huge.

- **Go to at least one networking event each week**.
  It doesn't matter if it's an after-work professional association meeting, a lunch and learn, or a running club, just make a commitment to get out and socialize consistently, make new friends, and talk about your passions on a regular basis.

Fear #2: I'm worried about money.

There are two flavors of this concern, the first being that you'll need to take a cut in pay in order to have a job that is fulfilling. That very well may be true. Although not as significant of a drop in income as I feared, it was the case for me when I left consulting for industry. But I enjoyed my job more, worked fewer hours, and was able to enjoy other parts of my life. I had the time and energy to take big trips and explore the world, to focus on my love life, and to learn to cook. I was way happier and more fulfilled than I could ever have been in consulting.

If you find yourself struggling with the idea of earning less money, I suggest revisiting your definition of success, as well as the personal costs of your current job. And if you decide the money is enough to keep you there, that's fine. Only you know what is most important when it comes to your happiness and fulfillment.

The second money concern I see most often is related to leaving your job. Maybe you were laid off or feel like you have no choice but to quit. While I'm not recommending quitting, I'm also not *not* recommending it. It all depends on your situation. I had to quit my consulting job in order to change careers, because between the travel and crazy hours, I simply did not have time to network or make meetings or interviews.

Solution: Understand your expenses and find new sources of cash.

Before you can solve for potential money issues, you need to understand your expenses – both current and the bare minimum you need to survive. Maybe you already track this, but for many of us (financial professionals included), this is an area that goes untouched. As a top source of stress for most adults, it's understandable if you've avoided the topic of finances up to this point. But if you want to change your career for the better, it's time to man (woman) up and face the numbers. After developing your baseline budget, you'll look for ways to save more, cut expenses and find new sources of income.

- **Determine your number and build a plan**.
  Figure out how much money you need to maintain your current lifestyle, and also to just get by, but still be comfortable. It might be less than you think. You've probably heard of the of the *Journal of Positive Psychology* study done about ten years ago where they found happiness does not increase with income once you hit $75,000. That's about $85,000 in 2017 dollars, but still less than you might think.

  To determine your number, first look at your expenses. It might help to use a service like Mint, or, to keep it even more simple, review credit card statements and keep track of all cash transactions for a week to track where your money is going. Next, review your current lifestyle and find places where you can cut expenses, even if temporarily. Draw up a budget that includes your "Must Haves" (rent, utilities, food, insurance, etc.) and your "Nice to Haves" (vacations, dinners out, massages, etc.). This will be different for everyone.

  Take Sue, a dear friend of mine who decided to quit her high stress job in Big Pharma in New York City to build her own online gifting business. She had saved up money before leaving, and to make it last even longer, found places to cut expenses. She colored her own hair rather than going to a salon. Instead of catching up with friends over expensive dinners, she met them for happy hour where there were specials on drinks and appetizers.

While she knew she had to be more thoughtful about where she spent her money, there were certain areas she chose not to skimp on. Sue maintained her gym membership because she knew that working out would keep her sane during this time of transition. And she always made sure to do what was necessary to look professional at interviews and networking events, which meant spending the money to dry clean her suits and buy a new pair of shoes.

After you've got your budget, you can build your escape plan with a timeline. If at all possible, I suggest having a minimum of six months, preferably 12 months, worth of "Must Have" dollars available to you before quitting. This can come from savings or other sources of cash discussed below.

- **Work part-time**.

  While it might not pay all the bills, working part-time while looking for a job has many benefits. It can give you more financial runway, keep your skills sharp, and make it easier to get out and network. There are many options beyond working at your local coffee shop (although that's fine too). Consulting firms like GLG and Business Talent Group make it easy for professionals to work with companies on a part-time, project basis. Or maybe you have other talents or skills that could earn you some extra cash in the short-term. For example, when I left consulting to change careers, in addition to freelance work with local start-ups, I was able to leverage my experience in teaching and take on a few one-on-one students while I looked for work.

- **Find other sources of cash**.
  Get creative about finding other sources of cash. In addition to dipping into your savings, you might be able to borrow from friends or family, take out a loan or cash out part of your 401K.

Fear #3: I'm not qualified.

You've probably heard various statistics around the idea that women are far less likely than men to apply for jobs where they don't meet all the qualifications. When this stat is quoted, it is often followed up with advice to just be more confident. Easier said than done. Beyond confidence though, it is common for people (especially perfectionists) to use lack of qualifications as an excuse to put off making a big, scary change. Only you know if that's true for you. It reminds me of one of my favorite quotes from Theodore Roosevelt,

Whenever you are asked if you can do a job, tell 'em, 'Certainly I can!' Then get busy and find out how to do it.

I love the spirit of that statement. Although the details of your situation will vary, I know that you are smart, persistent and resourceful. That's how you got to where you are now. And those qualities will help you get to the next level, as long as you don't let your fear (excuses) of qualifications get in the way.

Furthermore, whether the fear is real or imagined, there are a multitude of ways you can build up your knowledge, qualifications, and confidence. (Just don't let it stop you from taking action on your dreams.)

Solution: Find ways to learn and gain experience.

See Chapter 6, "Get Smart" for a more detailed discussion and examples of how to gain knowledge and experience. Depending on the nature of your career change, you may need to look into certifications or degrees. Unless you are changing to a profession in law or medicine, this is probably not the case. You can gain knowledge through research, talking to people in the industry, keeping up on the latest news, and taking free or fee-based classes. Experience can be achieved by volunteering for projects at work, for non-profits, or through consulting.

It's then your responsibility to articulate how your background, skills, and experience, both inside and outside work, make you a fit for your desired job. This is accomplished through developing a clear message and aligned personal brand, which is the basis for all your search activities, including networking and interviewing.

Fear #4: I'm worried about what my family/ friends/colleagues will think.

One of the biggest challenges people face is fear of judgment – from anyone and everyone. They worry that their parents will think they're irresponsible, that their friends will call them crazy, that their eighth grade crush whom they haven't spoken to in over ten years will see what a failure they are based on their LinkedIn profile.

It is reminiscent of the concern that some overweight people have when first going to the gym, the fear that everyone is going to stare or judge them because of how they look. But most people are so concerned with their own workout and their own bodies that they don't even notice. That same concept applies to a lot of the judgment we fear. Most people either aren't paying attention or don't care about our careers because they're spending their energy worrying about how their own success or lack thereof is perceived.

That said, those closest to us will likely have opinions when it comes to any big career changes. Perhaps it is even those opinions that led us to choose, or stay in, our unfulfilling job in the first place.

Solution: Have compassion, set boundaries, and limit contact.

The first step in overcoming this obstacle is to have compassion and understanding for well-meaning relatives and friends that are less than supportive of your goals. Most likely their opinions stem from their own fears and past experiences, and they just want the best for you – and think they know how to make that happen. But only you know what is true for you, and what you must do to go after the happiness and meaning you seek.

Nicole sought my advice when changing careers. Her mother was so worried, when her daughter quit her job as an investment banker to pursue a new career in advertising, that she insisted that they not tell her father for fear he would have a heart attack. It took about six months for Nicole to find a job, and the entire time, her mother questioned her about what she spent her money on, worried out loud that it was a big mistake to leave a great job in the current economy, and reminded her of all the reasons a company wouldn't hire an ex-banker to work in advertising. Despite all the negativity, Nicole knew that her mother meant well and that although it didn't always feel this way, her intentions were just to protect her daughter from her own regrets around career and money.

Intentions aside, Nicole recognized that she couldn't let her mother's harsh words and judgments derail her efforts or affect her mindset. To accomplish this, she had to set boundaries. In this case, that meant having an open, firm, and loving conversation with her mother. She let her know that while she appreciated her concern, this career change was important to her because she was unhappy and unfulfilled in her current job. Nicole allayed her mother's fears by sharing her strategy and plan to accomplish this goal, and assured her that if she needed any advice, she would ask. In the meantime though, she asked that the topic of career be off the table.

If you find the opinions or negativity of those closest to you is affecting your ability to focus and stay positive, you, too, may need to set boundaries. For people that you aren't as close with (or for family and friends that don't respect your boundaries), the easiest way to handle negativity might be to limit contact.

One of my favorite quotes is by Jim Rohn, who says that *you are the average of the five people you spend the most time with*. It definitely applies here. Whenever you're making a big change, it is helpful to surround yourself with people that are doing the same thing and having success, while also experiencing similar challenges. Spend more time with friends who lift you up and less time with those that don't.

Fear #5: I can't take the rejection.

I wish I could tell you there was a way around this one, but the fact is that rejection is just part of the process when looking for a new job or career. Depending on your past experiences, personality, and overall disposition, even the smallest perceived rejection can feel like a tragedy. But over time, your "rejection muscle" will get stronger. There's even a book on it. In *Rejection Proof*, Jia Jang actually went out of his way to be told "no" 100 days in a row. In doing so, he not only learned ways to get to a "yes," but perhaps more importantly, he built up his confidence and ability handle rejection.

Solution: Reframe rejection as feedback.

I'm not suggesting that you go out of your way to be rejected on a daily basis, but as with many challenges, mindset can make a huge difference here. It is unlikely that you're going to land the first job you go after, so rather than taking every "no" as a personal rejection, see it for what it is – feedback. Some of the feedback is useful and will help you refine your desires and message, while other feedback is just information telling you that a company, position or potential manager is not a good fit for you. In the latter case, the so-called rejection is actually saving you from another potentially toxic work environment. Or as the saying goes, sometimes *life's rejection is God's protection*.

Sometimes you'll think an interview went well and you won't hear back, or when you do, you'll be told they went in another direction. Try not to take it personally, because really – it's not. There could be any number of reasons for this – from your experience (too little or even too much) to organizational changes to lack of headcount approval. I've seen time and time again where people assume they did something wrong, when in reality the lack of an offer had nothing to do with them.

Take Carlo, the IT consultant from Chicago. After what seemed like a successful day of interviews and what was essentially a verbal offer from the owner, Carlo was shocked and disappointed when he didn't hear back and his emails and messages weren't returned. But months later, after he landed his current job, he received a call from the firm asking to pick up where they left off. They apologized for not being able to reach out sooner, and explained that they were in the midst of a merger and couldn't share that information or hire anyone until it was complete. Happy in his current role, Carlo was grateful that he didn't let what seemed like a rejection stop him from continuing his search and ultimately landing his dream job.

When you've done your homework, prepared and done your best, it does you no good to drive yourself crazy overanalyzing the situation. If you haven't heard back, follow up with the hiring manager periodically, expressing your continued interest in the position. Depending on your rapport with the hiring manager, you may also want to ask for feedback. Keep in mind though that for legal or other reasons, hiring managers will rarely be direct with you.

Although it will be hard in the moment, I encourage you to see each conversation, job application and interview as a gift – a way to learn more about yourself and what you want in your next job, and then to use this information to refine your message and job attraction strategy. This way, it's a constant feedback loop where every "no" gets you closer to not just any job, but the one that's right for you.

Early on in my quest to change from consulting to retail strategy, I remember interviewing with a top luxury department store's strategy team. I was excited about the opportunity, the brand and the possibility of working with a strong female-led team. Towards the end of each interview, I asked how success was measured. After all, if not tied to specific KPIs (key performance indicators), the success of a strategy could be a hard thing to measure.

The answer I got from each team member was the same. I was told that they knew they were doing a good job if the other leaders and teams liked them. They were a collaborative organization, and thus likeability was the top performance metric – even if that meant delaying and even foregoing important initiatives.

Maybe it was because I came from a consulting background where results were paramount, but to say I was shocked at this response would be an understatement. Of course, I understood that getting along with your colleagues is important, if not vital to the success of the organization. But to have likeability be the sole measure of success, and at the expense of progress, was not aligned with my desire to make a difference at one company. I didn't get the job, but even if I had been offered it, I would have declined for this reason. Not only did this rejection save me from a job that wasn't right for me, but it helped me to refine and articulate what I was seeking in my next role.

Fear #6: I'm afraid I'll fail. Maybe I'm not good enough.

Whenever we're doing something new or taking a risk, it is normal to fear failure and question your abilities. It would be weird if you *didn't* feel this way at least some of the time. And don't get me wrong – you will fail. But you will dust yourself off and try again until you are successful. That's part of being human, but you can't let it stop you from following your dreams.

In her book *Playing Big*, Tara Mohr dedicates an entire chapter to what she calls the "inner critic," that voice of self-doubt that even the most accomplished men and women hear, especially when leveling up in life. This voice is harsh, authoritative (and mean), and may sound like an old teacher or even your mother. Its evolutionary purpose is to protect us from the unknown, yet it can render us helpless.

Once we can recognize that voice, it might help to personify it (as someone outside of ourselves) and even have a conversation with it, telling it, "Thanks for your concern, but I got this." This technique may sound crazy at first, but after years of practice, I can vouch for its effectiveness. The reason it works is because in order to have a conversation with your inner critic, you have to acknowledge that it's not you; it's just a fear – a fear that you can overcome by taking action and proving it wrong.

Solution: Adjust your mindset and focus on what you can control.

I love how speakers reframe their anxiety before a big talk. Rather than think of it as fear, many of them have gotten into the habit of thinking of it as excitement. I have been told that when they feel their stomach in knots and their hands start to shake, they will literally talk to themselves (in their minds) and say, "Wow, I must be so excited about this presentation." This simple mindset change allows them to harness the nervous energy and use it for good – and can mean the difference between a lackluster presentation and an electrifying performance.

I'm not saying to ignore the fear. Go ahead, feel it, write about it in your journal, or tell a supportive friend. But then I challenge you to let it go, and follow the lead of speakers by using that energy for good. When you feel the fear, remind yourself that it's actually excitement for your new career and anticipation for the happiness and fulfillment you will feel from doing work that matters to you.

I am a big fan of the serenity prayer because it reminds us to focus on what we can control.

God, grant me the serenity to accept the things I cannot change,
Courage to change the things I can,
And wisdom to know the difference.

This is especially sound advice for anyone when looking for a job. Action is a great antidote to fear. Spend your time and energy on what you can control: your résumé, your online presence, your message, and your networking.

Finally, remind yourself why you are doing this. Regularly review your definition of success, your ideal day, and what staying in this position is costing you (all from Chapter 2). Write it on the mirror, put a post-it on your computer, and do anything that will keep your reasons for leaving top of mind.

No matter your fear, no matter the challenge, remember that you are in control. If you picked up this book, you're probably at a breaking point. If that's the case, then it's time to do something about it. No one is pushing you to do this. You've got to want it bad enough to overcome the challenges that come with making such a big change. I promise you though: The effort is well worth it. You deserve, and can have, a career that excites and inspires you, and the feeling of happiness and fulfillment that comes from meaningful work.

While this book is focused on career, we must also remember that as much as we might like to compartmentalize work from the rest of our lives, it is all connected. Especially during times of career transition, we can take comfort in knowing that we don't have to rely on our jobs to be our sole source of success, meaning, and happiness. I'm going to propose a radical idea here – that you deserve to have your work be just *one* of the many wonderful pieces of a full and satisfying life. Are you with me? If so, read on.

JOY NOTES

- You can overcome any challenge through mindset, planning and action.
- Action is the antidote to fear.
- Commit to the work, be prepared, and do your best. Trust in the process.
- Remember why you are doing this. Regularly review your definition of success and what staying in your current role is costing you.

CHAPTER EIGHT

It's My Life; It's Now or Never
Finding Meaning Outside of Work

*Don't get so busy making a living that you
forget to make a life.*
~ DOLLY PARTON

I f you've ever skipped plans with friends after work, and
instead opted for takeout and Netflix because of a bad day
at the office – or come home and started a fight with your
significant other after a particularly stressful day of meetings
– then you know how your work can affect the rest of your life.
The opposite is also true. No matter how wonderful a career
you have, it is difficult, if not impossible, to achieve happiness
and meaning if the rest of your life is empty or in turmoil.

When you picked up this book, you were no doubt focused on your problem at work. You likely asked yourself how you could be so unhappy when, by all outside measures, you had such a successful career. It just didn't make sense. And as you've seen, there are definite reasons for that, such as making decisions based on others' opinions and definitions of success, suffering the costs of not being true to your values, and not proactively taking control at work through boundaries, productivity, etc. But it would be a mistake to not also examine the rest of your life, as it's all connected.

The topic of work/life balance is an age-old and popular one, and for good reason. I do believe you can have it all, even if not all at the same time. I like the analogy that balancing all the different areas of life is like juggling. Many years ago, Bryan Dyson, then CEO of Coca Cola delivered Stanford University's commencement speech. In it, he said:

> *Imagine life as a game in which you are juggling five balls in the air. You name them – work, family, health, friends, and spirit – and you're keeping all of these in the air. You will soon understand that work is a rubber ball. If you drop it, it will bounce back.*

> *But the other four balls – family, health, friends, and spirit – are made of glass. If you drop one of these, they will be irrevocably scuffed, marked, nicked, damaged, or even shattered. They will never be the same.*

I read this to say that work is important, yes – but other areas of life are even more essential to our well-being, and when not cared for, can have detrimental consequences.

There are many ways to examine our lives outside of career. Below are the areas that come up most often, and need review, both for myself and with my clients:

- Family
- Friendships
- Romantic Love
- Health
- Spirituality
- Personal Growth
- Fun and Recreation

I also like the way Jonathan Fields approaches this topic in his book *How to Live a Good Life*. He breaks life into just three buckets:

- Contribution – how you bring your gifts and talents to the world, both in and outside of work
- Connection – with friends, family, significant others, yourself, and a higher power
- Vitality – the state of your mind and body

It's interesting that all areas of life listed above are related to relationships – whether with others, self, or a higher power. Harvard's Grant and Glueck 75-year study confirmed what many already believed – that relationships are the key to meaning and happiness in life. When these relationships are solid, they provide support to be successful in our careers. And just the opposite is just as true – when we are lacking in those areas, it is nearly impossible to be fulfilled at work.

So ask yourself: What are your top priorities in life – the areas that have the most meaning and bring the most happiness to you? Write them down and consider how healthy each area is, and how much time you devote to it. Is this in line with your stated priorities?

Let's think back to Catherine, the lawyer who had become burned out from working long hours at her New York City firm. She was very clear that in addition to work, health and finding love were her top priorities. Yet after she was done with her work, she did not have any energy or time left to commit to them. In fact, her work was a detriment to these areas – she had gained weight, gone on blood pressure medication, and was single (not by choice). Ultimately, she realized that her health and desire to have a family were far too important to continue on this path.

Catherine left her firm to work as the in-house attorney for a tech company, coincidentally just around the corner from her old office. With more reasonable hours and an in-office gym, it was easier to focus on her health and make time to date. Perhaps not surprisingly, less than two years after she made the move, she was married to the man of her dreams and training for her second marathon.

Your priorities are indicative of what you value – and what will bring you meaning and happiness. So, if like Catherine when I first began working with her, your actions are not aligned with your stated priorities, it's no wonder you're unhappy.

It's time to change that. Review the seven life categories above, and even add your own. Rate them each on a scale of 1-10, 1 being absolutely dissatisfied and 10 being perfectly content. Start by focusing on those areas that are below 5, choosing simple, measurable and actionable items to improve them. What can you do right now, and this week, to move one or two category scores up a point or more?

For example, when I find myself dissatisfied with health, I will make a concerted effort to sleep eight hours a night, workout three times a week, and limit dinners out to the weekends. If you're unhappy romantically, you might decide to go on one date a week, or if in a relationship, commit to a weekday and/or weekend date night. If you scored low on fun/recreation, plan to go to a movie, host a wine and puzzle night or finally explore the trails in your neighborhood park. Above all else, keep it fun and commit to making these areas of your life a priority - knowing that while it will help you with your career, the happiness you gain from improving other areas of your life is worth it, in and of itself.

Meaning can feel so elusive, but it's actually much more simple than you think. Here's the big secret – are you ready?

You already have it.

That's right. You don't need to look for meaning outside yourself. You play many roles in life, and they all contribute to the value you bring to the world. You're a daughter, a partner, a friend, a mentor. In *The Power of Meaning*, author

Emily Esfahani Smith reflects on meaning as "...not some great revelation. It's pausing to say hi to a newspaper vendor and reaching out to someone who seems down. It's... being a good parent or mentor to a child. It's sitting in awe beneath a starry night sky and going to a prayer service with friends. It's listening attentively to a loved one's story. It's taking care of a plant. These may be humble acts on their own. But taken together, they light up the world."

You are so much to so many people, in ways both big and small – ways in which you know, and ways in which you could never imagine. Listen to me when I tell you that you are needed and bring so much value to others already – just by being yourself.

This doesn't invalidate your desire to have a fulfilling career. You absolutely deserve that and can have it. But understand that you are already making a difference; you already have that inside you. And perhaps ironically, finding happiness and meaning in life outside of work, can actually lead to happiness and meaning at work. Not the other way around. It's time to move beyond just building a résumé and on to building a life you love - where success, meaning, and happiness in your career are but just one part of your amazingly fulfilling life.

JOY NOTES

- It's all connected. In addition to career – family, friendships, love, health and spirituality all contribute to your overall well-being.
- Relationships are essential to a happy and meaningful life.
- You are already meaningful, just as you are.
- You deserve, and can have success, meaning, and happiness in *all* areas of life.

CONCLUSION

Everything is okay in the end.
If it's not okay, then it's not the end.
~ UNKNOWN

Congratulations! By reading this book, you've taken the first step in your journey to career fulfillment. My hope for you is that through this process you've gained more self-awareness and can clearly articulate what is most important to you, so that you can have a career and life that you are proud of – and that makes you feel successful, happy, and on purpose. And along with that understanding, that you have clarity around your options and next steps to reach those goals.

In addition, I hope that you see that this process doesn't stop when you hit your goals. Once you're in a job that you love, it's easy to become complacent and focus on the day-to-day work at hand. But your dreams, priorities, relationships, and overall circumstances are all a moving target, which means that your goals of a few years ago – even a few months ago – may be slightly (or completely!) different today, and the steps needed to get there will need some adjusting.

For that reason, I urge you to set up a regular check-in with yourself to step back and look at the bigger picture – to review the various parts of your life and ask yourself the questions throughout this book related to your values, definition of success, and overall happiness. Without these periods of self-reflection, it is too easy to fall back into old habits and end up back where you started – unhappy, unfulfilled, and breaking down under the pressure of a life that you don't love. It would be great to plan quarterly check-ins, but even an annual review puts you ahead of most.

For years, I've made it a habit to do a review during the time between the holidays and New Year's, a time when life tends to slow down for me and I can make space to reflect. It's a tradition I've come to look forward to, as it allows me to regain the self-awareness necessary to stay (or get back) on track to living a life that makes me happy and fulfilled.

The ritual includes updating my résumé, reviewing accomplishments and disappointments in the past year, and planning ahead for the year to come. I look at each area of my life, from work to relationships to health, and ask myself if I am happy or if it needs more of my time and focus to get to that point. Then I build a plan – and actually, even a theme for the year – to make it happen.

Most importantly though, my wish for you is that you see what my 30-year-old self couldn't that night when she had a breakdown, and realized just how unhappy she was in her seemingly successful career and big city lifestyle. I want you to know, without a doubt, that everything you need is inside of you – to know that you don't need to search for meaning because you are already meaningful, just as you are. To realize you are in control of how you choose to view the story that is your life, and what actions you take to shape it. To know deep down that you have options and that no matter your experience (or lack thereof), your education, or your personal circumstance, it is never too late to make a change, big or small. And that even if there are naysayers (there will be), and even if it is really scary (it will be), and even if you sometimes want to give up (you will), that you will make it through to the other side - and not just survive, but come out a stronger, wiser, and more compassionate human being.

You've got this! Now go find your job joy!

Resources

Below are some of my favorite resources mentioned throughout the book.

The Happiness Hack: How to Take Charge of Your Brain and Program More Happiness Into Your Life, Ellen Petry Leanse

The Desire Map: A Guide to Creating Goals with Soul, Danielle LaPorte

Thrive: The Third Metric to Redefining Success and Creating a Life of Well-Being, Wisdom, and Wonder, Arianna Huffington

The Sleep Revolution: Transforming Your Life, One Night at a Time, Arianna Huffington

The Perfect Day Formula: How to Own the Day and Control Your Life, Craig Ballantyne

Quiet: The Power of Introverts in a World That Can't Stop Talking, Susan Cain

Playing Big: Practical Wisdom for Women Who Want to Speak Up, Create and Lead, Tara Mohr

How to Live a Good Life: Soulful Stories, Surprising Science, and Practical Wisdom, Jonathan Fields

The Power of Meaning: Finding Fulfillment in a World Obsessed with Happiness, Emily Esfahani Smith

While not specifically referenced, these books have helped shaped my way of thinking about happiness and fulfillment in work and life.

The Miracle Morning: The Not So Obvious Secret Guaranteed to Transform Your Life, Hal Elrod

The Big Leap: Conquer Your Inner Fear and Take Life to the Next Level, Gay Hendricks PhD

Start with Why: How Great Leaders Inspire Everyone to Take Action, Simon Sinek

Pulling Your Own Strings: Dynamic Techniques for Dealing with Other People and Living Your Life as You Choose, Wayne Dyer

Margin: Restoring Emotional, Physical, Financial and Time Reserves to Overloaded Lives, Richard Swenson

The Untethered Soul: The Journey Beyond Yourself, Michael A. Singer

A Year of Miracles: Daily Devotions and Reflections, Marianne Williamson

Acknowledgements

Mom and Dad, if you hadn't indulged my every reading and writing whim as a child, I'm sure *Job Joy* would still be just an idea, if that. I have fond memories of consuming a mountain of fresh books on every long road trip, spending many an afternoon at Barnes & Noble, and exploring little bookstores wherever we went, from the tiny used bookstore near ballet class to the hidden gem in Vermont where we debated – and even betted on – the correct form of the idiom "dead as a doornail." Still not sure who won that one...

And I would be remiss if I didn't mention all the time you spent with me in my even younger years, as I learned to read (I recall *Pompeii* and *King Tut* in the *Beginning to Read* series were favorites) or when you let me use your baby blue typewriter for all those hours at the kitchen table, where I would type (and retype) my stories over summer break, no doubt using up any correction tape in sight.

I love you so much and am so grateful to you for encouraging me to follow my passions from the very beginning.

Thank you John Scheyer, my love, for all your support during the book writing process... for celebrating every milestone with me, no matter how small – from finishing my first draft (of my first draft!), to pressing "send" on the final manuscript, and to reaching bestseller status during the ebook launch. Thank you for making sure I was surrounded by all my writing essentials – from snacks and my favorite teas, to flowers (and not just one bouquet!), to specially chosen inspirational quotes and of course, my "dare to be different" oakmoss sage-scented writing candle. I love you!

Special thanks to all my early supporters and readers of Job Joy, and especially those on my book launch team: Erin Bellis, Jess Box, Roni Carter, Karisa Deculus, Courtney Hunt, Morgan Husted, Shirley Pollock, Ellen O'Meara Kelly, Tanya Sanyal, Jessica Schiller Silverman, Shelly Sookraj, Hollie Tkac, Robin Quattlebaum, and Mara White. Thank you for sharing your career struggles so openly, for providing feedback on everything from covers to content, and for sharing the book with your friends. I so appreciate you!

Thank you Angela Lauria, book coach extraordinaire and founder of The Author Incubator. I appreciate your tough love, firm deadlines and overall guidance, all of which were integral in making *Job Joy* a reality.

And to the Morgan James Publishing team: Special thanks to David Hancock, CEO & Founder for believing in me and my message. To my Author Relations Manager, Gayle West, thanks for making the process seamless and easy. Many more thanks to everyone else, but especially Jim Howard, Bethany Marshall, and Nickcole Watkins.

About the Author

Kristen J. Zavo is a sought after international keynote speaker, career coach and corporate strategy professional. She

believes everyone deserves a career that excites and inspires them – and the feeling of happiness and fulfillment that comes from meaningful work. She has formally and informally helped thousands of readers, clients, colleagues, and friends find job satisfaction whether they chose to stay put, find a new job, or completely change careers.

While in college, Kristen discovered a love for teaching and presenting through her work with a leading test prep company, which she continued part-time for years into her career. After graduating, she began her professional career in investment banking before moving on to almost a decade in financial and strategic consulting. From there, she transitioned to industry where she focused on strategy, marketing, and customer experience for a top eyewear manufacturer and retailer. She has been featured in the Huffington Post and now speaks all over the world at conferences on business, marketing, and of finding joy at work.

Kristen earned her MBA with a concentration in finance from the John F. Welch College of Business at Sacred Heart University in Fairfield, Connecticut. She also has a Bachelor of Science in business administration with an emphasis in marketing plus a double major in psychology and a minor in mathematics. A lifelong learner, she has earned multiple professional designations over the course of her career, and is a certified Well Life Coach.

Kristen has a passion for world travel, especially to places with beautiful beaches. She's an avid reader, aspiring yogi, and skincare product junkie. She grew up on the east coast, has lived all over the U.S. and currently lives in Cincinnati, Ohio.

kristenzavo.com
kristen@findyourjobjoy.com

THANK YOU

Thank you so much for reading *Job Joy: Your Guide to Success, Meaning, and Happiness in Your Career*! If you've made it this far I know one of two things about you. First, you're more ready than ever to experience job joy. And second, maybe you also start at the end of the book before diving in (hey, me too!).

I would love to learn more about your journey and success in pursuing the career of your dreams. Please keep in touch! You can find and connect with me on LinkedIn, Facebook, Instagram and Twitter. Visit jobjoybook.com for a special surprise just for *Job Joy* readers.

Morgan James makes all of our titles available
through the Library for All Charity Organization.

www.LibraryForAll.org